EVERYTHING WE PROMISED

KATE SMITH

COPYRIGHT © 2016 KATE SMITH

This book is a work of fiction. Names, characters, places, and incidents are either the product of the author's imagination or are used fictitiously, and any resemblance to actual persons, living or dead, business establishments, event, or locales is entirely coincidental.

All rights reserved. No part of this book may be reproduced, scanned, or distributed in any printed or electronic form without permission. Please do not participate in or encourage piracy of copyrighted material in violation of the author's rights.

KateSmithAuthor.com

Paperback ISBN: 978-1-9993893-5-2
E-book ISBN: 978-0-9953487-8-3

Cover: Ana Chabrand Design House

So this was how it ended ...

Prologue

Tiffany

TIFFANY'S ENTIRE WORLD CHANGED AT the moment of her first real kiss. And not one of those quick pecks from a nervous teenage boy, either, but a long, deep, bordering on passionate, embrace. When it happened, it was a complete surprise, as the awkward, shy girl with the cascade of honey-blonde hair and big blue eyes failed to attract the boys at her previous school. It seemed history might repeat itself at the prestigious boarding school she attended as a scholarship student.

Tiffany hated her new school. The lack of privacy in her shared dorm room. Her less-than-friendly roommate. The communal meals. The strict timetable. And she mourned the loss of her closest friends. They celebrated birthdays and attended parties while she slogged through the day among Chicago's elite. Or at least their offspring.

Then everything changed. Her grouchy dorm mate dropped out over the Christmas break. To her surprise, the ultra-popular Alexis Carr, known as Alex by her friends, moved into the shared room. Blessed with a sunny disposition and an infectious laugh, the gregarious Alex often invited Tiffany to sit with her group at meals.

Tiffany learned to keep her head down, too timid to speak. When a certain adorable dark-haired teenage boy joined the raucous group, she became positively tongue-tied.

Accepting the invitation to sneak from the dorms—something Alex and her posse did regularly—was impossible. Tiffany would never risk embarrassing herself in front of her secret crush.

One Friday evening in late April, it all changed.

Alexis cast a glance over her shoulder. "We're hanging out tonight." The girl dragged a brush through her dark, silky hair. "Care to join us, Tiffany?"

"Won't the others mind?"

"Of course not. Besides, do you want to pass up the chance to hang out with you know who?" Alex grinned. "You think he's cute. Admit it."

She ducked her head. "Aren't you two involved?"

"No way. We're friends. We've never dated or anything." Her roommate shrugged. "Well, he kissed me once, but only after Tom dared him. Aiden's the sweetest, but it felt like kissing my brother."

Tiffany wrinkled her nose. "You don't have any siblings."

"That's not the point." Her friend waved a hand. "Every time I invite you out, you say no, yet you're crushing on the guy. Hard. If you hang with us, you can talk to him instead of performing covert surveillance."

Her cheeks flamed. Had the teenage boy noticed how she stared at him? "He'd never be interested."

"Don't be delusional." Alex frowned, taking Tiffany by the shoulders and steering her toward the mirror. "You're gorgeous." Her friend lifted Tiffany's long blonde locks. "Look at this hair."

"What about the other girls? He has his pick."

"They have nothing on you." Her friend rested her hands on her hips, leaning in and lowering her voice. "Can I tell you a secret?"

Tiffany nodded.

"He's fascinated by the new girl. If you come, I'll ensure you get alone time." Alex wiggled her brows. "I have the power."

"No." She shook her head. "He never says a word. Not to me."

"When he tries to talk to you, you blow him off. He assumes you're unavailable. Or worse. Uninterested."

"You're teasing," Tiffany whispered.

"There's a simple way to find out." Alex studied her for a moment, pursing her lips. "You can't go like that." She flicked a hand at Tiffany's sweatpants and hoodie. "Change and touch up your makeup. We leave half an hour after lights out."

That evening, at her roommate's insistence, Tiffany joined the other girls and exited through the dorm window, her knees trembling as she scrabbled down the rough brick face, clinging to small window ledges.

What if someone caught them, and she had to endure her father's wrath? Or what if Aiden rejected her?

None of that happened. She had an amazing night, and when the first light of dawn streaked the sky, Aiden hung back and walked with her.

"Why haven't you come before?" He studied her with those sparkling brown eyes.

"I'm never invited." She shuffled through the grass, heat rising in her cheeks.

"That's a blatant lie." His gentle smile took the edge off of the words. "Consider yourself invited." He smirked. "Now I see you possess the power of speech."

She turned her head and swiped at the tear trickling down her cheek, hoping he wouldn't realize how his off-hand comment affected her.

"Hey." He grabbed her hand, forcing her to a halt. "I'm only teasing, Tiffany. Don't cry."

Her breath hitched as he swiped a thumb across her cheek, brushing away the salty drops. She stared into his eyes, mesmerized and powerless to blink or avert her gaze.

"You're sweet."

"I'm a mess. Why waste your time? Plenty of girls are begging for your attention." She tilted her head. "What do you want from me?"

He narrowed his eyes. "What? You think I'm one of those guys? Is that why you refuse to talk to me?" Aiden headed toward the dorms. "Whatever."

"No. I didn't mean …" Tiffany hurried to catch up. "Aiden."

"What?" He stopped and spun to face her. "I'm not oblivious. People assume things about me, but I never realized you thought that way."

"I don't." She picked at her nail. "I'm a scholarship student, and you're a Hamilton. Everybody recognizes you and your family, but nobody knows me. I'm a nothing."

"You're not nothing." He cupped her cheek in his palm. "Relax. Let people get to know you." His smile sent her pulse racing. "I had fun. Will you come next time?"

"I'm not like you or your friends."

"Who cares? We don't. Anyway, how many times are you thirteen and responsibility free?" The corners of his luscious mouth twitched.

The strangeness of that phrase coming from a teenage boy made her giggle.

"Yeah, you laugh." A heart-stopping grin appeared. "My future is laid out in a perfect road map. I'm having fun while I still can." The smile faded as he stepped closer. "Tiffany?" The low timbre of his sweet voice uttering her name sent a shiver coursing down her spine.

He leaned in, his breath wafting across her skin before he captured her lips in the gentlest of kisses. His warm soft mouth against hers created a stirring in her belly. The brush of his fingertips on her cheek made her knees tremble, and she almost melted. "I've been dying to do that," he said in a low voice before he kissed her again.

She closed her eyes, her fingers twining through his thick silky hair. She'd imagined the moment of her first kiss, but this exceeded expectations. Her thoughts jumbled, heat rising up her neck and into her cheeks at the involuntary, throaty moan that slipped out.

His arm curled around her waist, drawing her closer as his hand cradled her cheek, the tip of his tongue tracing hers. A moment later, he pulled away, his dark eyes half-closed as he bestowed a sultry, mind-shattering smile. "Mmm."

Her cheeks burned. "Sorry," she whispered as she tucked her chin to her chest. "I've never ..." *Shut up.* "You think I'm an awful kisser."

A brow rose as a rueful smile appeared, his head shaking in a subtle motion. "That's not what I was thinking, but we'd better get back." He reached for her hand.

Those precious minutes shared in the dim light of dawn inextricably intertwined her future with Aiden Hamilton's. Her entire world changed at the moment of her first kiss.

Chapter 1

Aiden

A boy's shrill voice pierced the air several rows behind Aiden as the aircraft bumped across the tarmac toward the O'Hare terminal. "Mommy. We're home."

Home. Aiden pinched the bridge of his nose, blinking against the burn. He wished he could join the other passengers emerging from flight-induced stupors, smothering smiles, and tapping at chiming phones.

Chicago was simply a distant memory, blurred over three years of exile. He was sorry he was back.

Excited chatter rolled over him as they rolled to stop, and he rose and stretched to work out the kinks. After a moment, he tugged his carry-on from the overhead bin.

He slung his bag over his shoulder and trudged through the jetway, gazing around as he wandered along the concourse, in no hurry to reach the baggage area. By the time he arrived, most of the passengers were already in the arms of their loved ones, and the animated calls and murmurs of family members flowed around him.

"I missed you." A teenage girl threw herself into the arms of an older woman he assumed was her mother.

Aiden turned away from the happy scenario and shuffled toward the carousel. He found a vacant spot and leaned against a pillar, tipping his head back and closing his eyes, blocking out the small but joyful reunions continuing around him.

"Mr. Hamilton?"

Aiden glanced at the uniformed man. "That's me."

"Can I retrieve your bag, sir?" The man's brows lifted.

Aiden motioned to the black case with the distinctive red baggage tag as it slid from above and landed with a soft thunk on the conveyor. "That one."

The man maneuvered through the gathering crowd, scooped up the bag, and wound his way back. "Ready, sir?"

Aiden followed the man to the sleek black sedan and waited for the driver to open his door. *Funny how old habits remained second nature even after all this time.* He settled in the leather seat as the driver stowed his bag.

Moments later, the car pulled from the curb and merged into traffic. He closed his eyes, concentrating on calming his thoughts and relaxing his tense muscles.

Finally, the car slowed and turned through the familiar iron gates. The sedan drew to a smooth stop in the circular drive.

Aiden inhaled a long slow breath as the driver opened his door. "Thank you." He stared at the imposing stone mansion. Nothing had changed. The vines still crept up the South wall, the fountain bubbled merrily in the center of the circular drive, the flowerbeds overflowed with bright blooms, and the lawns were a lush and immaculate green. Even the most meticulous greens keeper would be envious.

The massive wooden doors swung open the moment he set foot on the first step. "Hi, Bernard." He shrugged out of his light coat.

Bernard draped the jacket over his arm. "Welcome home, sir." He nodded before extending his arm toward the study. "Mr. Hamilton requested you report to him upon arrival."

Aiden lifted his chin and tilted his head, listening for sounds of life. *Silence.* Nobody appeared, but this wasn't a surprise. Expecting an enthusiastic or warm welcome for the errant grandson was ridiculous.

"Sir?"

"Thank you, Bernard." He trudged across the gleaming tile. Requested? No. *Summoned.* That was more accurate. And it would be unwise to keep Thomas Hamilton waiting.

Aiden proceeded down the marble-tiled hallway and tapped on the door before entering the dark-paneled room.

The gray-haired man behind the desk fixed a cold gaze on Aiden, not bothering to rise from the leather chair behind the oak desk. He tapped the nib of his pen against the paper, barely blinking as he stared at his grandson.

"Grandfather." Aiden straightened, maintaining a level tone and expressionless visage even as the bitter hatred rose. He longed to vent his rage upon this imperious man, but he bit back the scathing words.

The memory of the last time he'd stood in this spot flooded into his mind and it felt like he was right back to that day. As he had then, he fixed his eyes on the painting behind Thomas's head and clenched his jaw. He forced his hands to relax, doing his utmost not to curl them into fists.

"Dinner will be served at seven sharp." Thomas tapped the manila envelope sitting on the side of his desk twice with the tip of his index finger. "This contains the information on your apartment. Be packed and ready to leave by next Thursday."

Aiden translated this as he smothered the scoff. *Be sure you're out of my house by next Thursday.* That's what the man really meant.

There would be little packing to complete. Even as he stood here, the upstairs maid would be unpacking his bag, sorting his laundry, and boxing up the souvenirs he'd brought home.

That same maid would repack his bags and, he was sure, his few belongings would be on their way to Philadelphia before he left Chicago.

His grandfather narrowed his eyes and pushed the package across the expanse of the oak desk. After a moment of intense scrutiny, the man bent his head and focused on his paperwork. He waved toward the door. "That's all."

Aiden took one step forward to retrieve the information before leaving the room as silently as he'd entered. He headed down the hallway and exited through the French doors at the rear of the house.

It was pointless to head to his room. Instead, he crossed the lawn and slipped into the cool depths of the pool house before pulling out his phone and using his speed dial to make the call.

"Hey. How are you?" Tom asked. "Where are you?"

"Chicago. At least for now." Aiden dropped onto the couch and propped his feet on the coffee table.

"Your grandparents' house?"

"Unfortunately."

"You want to break out?"

"I'd better stick around for dinner, but after they've gone to bed, I'll escape."

"We're heading to the beach later. Do you want me to pick you up?"

Aiden debated on his answer. Having a ride would make things easier, but he had another stop to make. "No. Maybe I'll meet you there, but if not, then tomorrow night for sure. I can't wait to see everybody."

"We're happy you're finally back."

Once he'd finished his call with Tom, he decided to work out and do some laps in the pool. He needed to keep himself occupied, or he'd go crazy.

Hours later, after an excruciating formal dinner, Aiden retreated to his room and flopped onto his bed, covering his eyes with the back of his hand. His grandparents had acted as if nothing had changed. They hadn't inquired about his travels or time overseas. Aside from a light kiss on his cheek from his grandmother, his absence hadn't been acknowledged.

In one short week, he'd move to Philadelphia, and his grandparents could go on as if he'd never been here at all.

He turned on the big screen television affixed to the wall and flipped through the channels. Nothing to do but bide his time. His grandfather insisted on retiring to his room on a strict and predictable schedule, so he'd only have an hour to kill.

By ten-thirty, the house was dark and silent. Aiden crept into the hallway and tiptoed toward the back staircase. Nobody seemed to be around, but one could never tell in this house. His grandparents maintained a large staff, including at least two maids who had a habit of popping up from nowhere. But he supposed no one would prevent him from leaving. He'd turned eighteen in June. A grown up. No longer a child to be ordered about.

Aiden longed to escape the heavy and oppressive atmosphere in this mausoleum. The keys on the rack just inside the garage door beckoned him, and he selected a set without hesitation. The buttery, soft leather welcomed him as he slid into the driver's seat and gripped the wheel, giving a light tap on the garage door opener.

A grin spread across his face as the engine purred to life. After easing the car out of the garage, he navigated the dimly lit drive without the headlights. Once he turned onto the main road, he flicked them on and retracted the convertible's roof. A satisfying roar rose from the precision engine as Aiden pressed the accelerator to the floor. *Ahhh, freedom at last.*

His grandfather would have a coronary if he caught Aiden driving his pride and joy, but ... *What the hell?* What could Thomas Hamilton do to him that he hadn't already done?

The luxurious seat suited Aiden, but he grimaced at the jarring country twang that poured from the high-end sound system. "That man still has no taste in music." He stabbed at the controls on the steering wheel and tapped along to an upbeat rock song as he savored the warm evening air sweeping over him.

As he neared his destination, he lowered the volume to a whisper and slowed to a crawl. The smoke-gray sports car blended into the shadows left between the scattered streetlights on this peaceful residential avenue. *Perfect.* No need to disturb the neighbors.

Most of the houses were quiet with darkened windows, signaling the occupants had retired for the evening, including the ones inside the stately colonial home.

After a quick scan of the street, he hopped from the car and trotted down the verge of grass along the sidewalk before veering across the lush green lawn. The familiar trellis beckoned him, and he tugged at it, hoping it wouldn't break free from its anchors when he added the weight of his muscular six foot frame.

The creak of aged wood had him holding his breath as he scaled it one inch at a time. A sigh escaped as he clung to the ledge. Fortunately, the window was open a crack to allow the cool night air into the bedroom.

"Tiff," he whispered as he tapped on the glass. "Wake up."

A rustle came from the direction of the bed, followed by shuffling feet. "Who's there?"

"Tiff. It's me. Hurry up, my fingers are cramping."

"Aiden?" A pale face appeared at the window. The girl's eyes widened as she opened the window further. "You're here. When did you get back?" Tiffany reached out, tugging at him as he slid through the window and landed on the floor with a slight thump. She threw a panicked look over her shoulder. "Shh."

"Get dressed," he whispered. "Come for a ride with me."

"I don't know." She hesitated and glanced toward her door.

"I haven't seen you in forever, Tiff. Please?"

"Shush, they'll hear you. I'll be down in a minute." She motioned him away, still throwing anxious looks toward her bedroom door.

Aiden lowered himself to the ground, stepping into the shadows as he waited. The scrabble of feet against wood alerted him and held up his hands, supporting her as she climbed down.

As soon as her feet touched the grass, she threw her arms around him. "I thought you were never coming home."

Aiden rocked her against his chest. "I'm sorry. I didn't have a choice." A sweet floral scent surrounded him as he buried his face in her hair. Being in her arms made him feel like he was finally home.

"It's been years." Red-rimmed shimmering eyes scanned him as she offered a faint smile. "You're so tall. Mmm," she said as she ran her fingertips over his firm chest, "and muscly."

"Let's get out of here before someone sees." He linked their fingers and tugged her toward the car.

"You're going to be in so much trrrrrouble." A grin spread across her face as she sang out the final word. "Does your grandfather know you have his Porsche?"

"Are you kidding? You know how he is about his cars." Aiden rolled his eyes even as his lips twitched. "He'll never know." He opened her door.

Tiffany smothered a giggle as Aiden guided that car along a familiar and winding route toward their favorite spot by the lake.

As soon as he shut off the car, Tiffany turned toward him. "How have you been? I can't believe you're here." She brushed her fingertips over his cheek. "It's so good to see your face."

"You got my letters?"

"Alex smuggled them to me." Her vibrant blue eyes shone with tears.

Aiden cupped her face in his palms. "It's so good to be here."

They stared at each other for a moment, before their lips met. At first, it was tender and gentle, but it grew, becoming deeper and more passionate.

"Aiden," she murmured as she slid her hands under his shirt, pressing herself against him.

He pulled her closer, luxuriating in the feel of her soft lips on his, plundering her mouth. This visit might seem impulsive, but he couldn't stand another day without seeing her. With her in his arms again, the pain of missing her faded away. He couldn't let go.

"Back seat?" he whispered before capturing her sweet mouth again.

She nodded.

Aiden tumbled over the seat, and then lifted Tiffany, encouraging her to join him.

"Aiden." She giggled as she landed on top of him.

"Shh." He wrapped his arms around her, kissing her as he spanned her tiny waist with his hands.

Tiffany slid a leg over, straddling him. She peered into his eyes and ran her fingers through his hair. "I can't believe you're here."

"Me either." He tangled his hand in her honey-blonde hair and pulled her to him, nuzzling against her neck.

Tiffany leaned back enough to peel her shirt off, then pressed her mouth to his.

Aiden returned her fiery kisses, his heart pounding as he caressed her soft skin. With a flick, he unhooked her bra and tossed it aside, burying his face against her.

"Love me," she whispered against his hair.

⁓

As he cuddled with Tiffany on the leather seat, he rested his cheek against her silky hair and savored the feel of her in his arms.

She sighed and snuggled against his chest. "I forgot how amazing we are together."

He dropped a kiss on her temple and closed his eyes, refusing to think about the others who'd been in their lives during their forced separation. He brushed his fingertips up and down her arm. "You're not seeing anyone, right?"

Tiffany shook her head. "No." She blinked her shiny eyes. "Can we not talk about it? We agreed, Aiden. You were gone so long."

"I know." He kissed her lips. "Tiff?"

"What?"

"Have you thought about Philly?"

"What about it?"

"So you didn't get it? I'm moving next week for medical school."

"You only came home."

"Come with me."

"To Philly?" A frown settled on her face. "And do what?"

"Go to school?" Aiden grasped her arms. "Please, Tiff? We've been apart for so long, and you know I've always wanted to be a doctor."

"Dr. Aiden Hamilton." She brushed his hair back from his forehead. "That has a beautiful ring to it." She bit her lip. "I can't. I start classes at the Art Institute next week."

Aiden's heart sank. His hard work over the past three years had paid off, and now his dream to attend medical school had come true. Would he be forced to live without Tiffany? He'd anticipated this moment for so long. Having her in his arms with the knowledge they'd be parted so soon was bittersweet.

Tiffany relaxed against his chest and sighed. "Will we ever be together?"

"We can visit. Long distance relationships aren't ideal, but here we are after three years. Can we try?"

"Philly is much closer than wherever you happened to be overseas on any given day. Do you think it will work? My dad …"

"You'll be eighteen at the end of September. What can he say?"

"He could refuse to pay my tuition. I only have a small scholarship, and if he takes away his support, I can't go. It's all I've ever wanted."

"We'll find a way. We've kept secrets before, Tiffany. What's one more?"

"Please, don't." She pressed her face into his chest and sniffled. "I can't even talk about it. Please don't make me relive it."

"Hey." Wrapping his arms around her, he held her tight. It had been even more difficult for her than it had for him, but he shared her pain. "We don't have to talk about it, honey, but I love you, and I want us to be together. Will you consider it? Maybe I should apply for medical school in Chicago."

"You can't give up your spot. It's a great school. Besides, how could you live in the same house as your grandfather?"

Aiden stared at the stars as silence fell over them. It seemed an impossible situation. Whenever they managed to find their way back into each other's arms, they were torn apart. He'd loved this girl forever, but now he'd have to leave her all over again.

He let his eyes slide shut and snuggled her against him, wishing everything was different.

Chapter 2

Tiffany

TIFFANY SETTLED BETWEEN THE SHEETS and pressed her fingertips against her lips. The memory of her tryst with Aiden and accepting his passionate kisses caused a heat to rise within her. What they'd shared at fifteen ... that was nothing compared to how he made her feel now. The way he held her, loved her, and his tender caresses made her weep and beg for more.

She closed her eyes, envisioning Aiden's hot body against hers. He'd grown and matured in his time away, his firm muscles telling her a tale of an active life overseas. The secret postcards she'd received from all over the world documenting his travels still seemed unreal. For her, his life-altering experiences were impossible to understand.

Aiden appearance at her window had been a complete shock. Nobody had mentioned his return. Of course, it was summer so most of her friends were at the Vineyard. Maybe they didn't know? With Alex gone, she'd received nothing from Aiden for the entire summer. He'd said he sent a letter.

She sighed as she contemplated her bleak life and the haze of boredom that had consumed her over the past two months. After that fateful year she'd turned fifteen, her parents banned future visits to the Vineyard. Her father directed his anger toward Alex's parents, blaming their lax supervision. A ridiculous, intolerant attitude from Tiffany's viewpoint, since the Carrs had nothing to do with any of it.

Once David Baxter laid down the law, arguing was futile. So every summer her two best friends, Alexis Carr and Jenna Maxwell, joined their families on a magical holiday in the Vineyard while Tiffany wasted away in Chicago. Or she visited boring relatives with her mother or traveled with her parents as her father glad-handed slimy and pompous politicians. She'd learned to smile and act the part of the perfect and obedient daughter, keeping her opinions to herself.

If only she could escape to Philadelphia with Aiden. She'd missed him so much her entire body ached. Tears rose to her eyes. In one short week, he'd leave again. How could she bear another four long years stuck here without him?

She twisted and turned, struggling to find a comfortable position despite repeated attempts at plumping her pillow. Her mind refused to shut down. Every time she closed her eyes, she pictured him.

⁓≺

Tiffany rolled and fumbled for her ringing phone, her mind groggy from lack of sleep.

"I'm baaaaaaaack." Alexis sang down the line.

"How was it?" Tiffany stretched and blinked her gritty eyes.

"Great. Joel and I spent almost every day together," Alex said. "I'm sorry, I'm a rotten friend. You were stuck here. What did you do?"

"Nothing exciting, I promise. We visited my horrible Aunt Harriet in Portland, and I acted the part of the perfect daughter. What else?" Tiffany shuddered at the thought of staying at her aunt's home. The woman never expressed any sort of affection and stared at her with an icy gaze. Damaged goods. That's what she was to Harriet Baxter.

"Why wouldn't your parents allow you to visit our beach house for even a week?"

Familiar nausea rose. Tiffany pressed the back of her hand against her mouth, smothering the sob. A single tear trickled down her face, but she brushed it away.

"No one will talk about it. Everyone clams up when I mention a visit. What happened, Tiffany?"

"We have to set a good example." She forced a cheery tone to her voice. "My father's political aide laid down the law on the family togetherness agenda."

"Huh." Alex snorted out the word. "Stupid, leaving you marooned in Chicago the whole damn summer."

"Aiden came home," Tiffany whispered, unable to keep the news from spilling from her mouth.

"What? When?"

"Yesterday. He's here for a week, and then he's gone. He's moving to Philadelphia. Did you know?" Tiffany twirled a strand of hair around her fingertip. "I get him back, only to lose him again."

"Holy crap. He got into Penn?" Alex asked. "He'll be Ivy League. Dr. Hamilton. Can you imagine?"

"It's not so hard to believe. He's brilliant, and he completed his undergrad at Oxford." Tiffany flopped against her pillow. "How he got his grandfather to agree, I'll never know."

"It was his grandmother. She's a softie when it comes to Aiden." Alex sighed. "Lucky guy. Three years of traveling overseas between terms at Oxford. The postcards made me green. All the places he's been and the things he's done."

"I missed him." Tiffany paced to the window, wishing he'd reappear. To her, experiences meant nothing. They were simply dark memories that required burying deep inside her mind. "I thought when he came home, he'd truly be here, but he's running off to Philadelphia."

"Attending school isn't running off."

"It's all the same to me because he won't live in Chicago." Her parents would rather die than allow her to make a single trip to Philadelphia on her own. "You're leaving soon, aren't you?"

"Yes," Alex said. "Joel starts his undergrad in September. I don't know how we'll manage being apart."

Tiffany sniffled as she wondered the same thing about her and Aiden.

"Up." Her mother poked her head in the door several hours later. "You've been lounging around all morning. Take a shower."

"Fine." Tiffany snatched her robe from the end of her bed and pushed past her mother into the hallway.

"Enough attitude, young lady. You've been moping around the house all summer."

"Maybe because it's boring. I wish you let me go to the beach with Alex and Jenna."

"Why?" Her mother crossed her arms and narrowed her eyes. "So you can get yourself into trouble?"

Tiffany dropped her chin to her chest, fighting the tears that sprang to her eyes. She scurried into the bathroom and slammed the door before sinking onto the toilet. A pictured formed of the disgust her father displayed the day her mother had dragged her into the office. Nothing Tiffany had ever done seemed to satisfy the man, and that day, she'd proven to be a complete disappointment to her family.

She cupped a hand over her belly, taking several deep breaths and pushing down the emptiness lingering inside. Aiden gave her everything missing in her life, but they sent him away.

A sharp rap sounded on the door. "Hurry up in there."

Tiffany stripped off her clothes and tossed them into the hamper before stepping under the spray, wrapping her arms around herself.

"Fifteen minutes, young lady."

Tonight. She only had to wait a few more hours.

The loud voices faded away, but she remained frozen and wrapped in silence, her blanket over her ears and back to the door.

In this position, it was easier to ignore her mother's nightly intrusion into her room. To feign sleep so her parents would let down their guard and leave her be. The constant vigilance on her whereabouts was wearing. She could barely pee or take a shower without her mother tracking her down.

Tonight, the visit didn't come. She assumed they were otherwise occupied. She grimaced, blocking the repugnant thought from her mind. How her mother tolerated that man's touch, she never understood.

It afforded her some rare peace as she watched the bright red numbers on the digital clock advance minute by minute until ten forty-five. They must be asleep by now.

Tiffany crept from her bed and through the open window, down the trellis, culminating in a mad dash across the lawn. This dodging from shadow to shadow brought back memories. The many times she'd crawled out windows in the dark of night.

A hand snaked out of the blackness under the elm tree, propelling her against a firm warm body. Fingers clamped over her mouth at her startled yelp, replaced moments later with demanding lips. The rough bark of the trunk dug into her back through her light blouse as the man pressed her against the tree, devouring her mouth.

The familiar masculine scent and taste of his tongue sent her pulse skyrocketing. "Aiden." She forced out his name in a breathless whisper and tipped her head to the side, a moan escaping as his lips grazed the sensitive spot on her neck.

His warm breath wafted against her flesh, causing goosebumps down her arms. "Shh. You'll wake the neighborhood." he whispered.

"Then let's go where nobody will hear."

"Good idea. What took you so long?"

"My parents had a ... discussion."

"Another one, huh?" Aiden snorted. "I don't know how your mom tolerates him."

"Let's not talk about it." She looked away and blinked hard. "It's a waste of time. He'll never change."

"It's bad?" Aiden squeezed her hand. "You can tell me. I won't say anything to anyone, I promise."

"Let's have some fun, please?" She forced a smile and batted her eyes at him. "Everyone is at the beach."

Aiden tipped his head as he entwined his fingers with hers. "Have it your way, but I'm here if you need to talk." He led her toward a red BMW convertible and opened the passenger door.

"Wow." She smoothed her skirt as she slid into the leather seat. "Steal another of your grandfather's cars?"

"This is mine. They delivered it today. My belated birthday gift and transportation out of town. The faster I leave, the better, I guess."

Tiffany angled her body toward him as they drew away from the curb. "A new car." She curled a hand around the back of his neck, swirling her fingers through the hair at the nape. "You know what that means?"

A smile twitched at the corners of his mouth as he caressed her leg with his fingertips. "What?"

"We'll be late to the party," she whispered as she leaned closer, nibbling at his earlobe. "Take me to our spot."

"You're late." Jenna scampered toward them and threw her arms around Tiffany for a long hug. She turned to Aiden. "Look what washed up on the beach."

Aiden smirked, but snatched Jenna off of her feet and twirled her around. "Good to see you, Jenn."

"It's been far too long." She held him at arm's length, tipping her head back. "You're so tall. The pictures you took with Tom were, what, a year ago?"

"He joined me in Spain for two weeks last summer. Where is—"

"Aiden." Alex's voice rang out and their friend dashed across the sand, her dark hair fluttering in the light breeze sweeping in from the lake. "I missed you, honey." She leaped at Aiden, wrapping her arms around his neck.

Aiden's deep laugh sent a delightful shiver through Tiffany. It all seemed so normal and comfortable. The gang together again.

Tom, Joel, and Ryan appeared from down the beach.

"The long-lost traveler." Tom clapped Aiden on the back. "How long are you staying?"

"I leave on Thursday for Philly. What did you decide?"

"Yale." Tom grinned. "I'll only be a couple of hours drive from you."

Joel smiled. "University of Chicago."

"Stanford." Ryan mock saluted.

Tiffany half-registered the conversation as the guys cracked open bottles and discussed their plans.

"So …." Jenna nudged her in the ribs and pulled her aside. "How are things with Aiden? You came with him?"

"That I did." Tiffany forced the smirk from her face. "It's good, except for the part where he leaves again." She glanced at the group of guys and lowered her voice. "He asked me to move to Philadelphia."

"He did?" Jenna's eyes widened. "Are you going?"

"How can I? My father will freak. If I go, he'll refuse to pay my tuition."

"Three years you've been apart." Jenna tapped a finger against pursed lips. "Don't rush. Anyway, you're starting at the Art Institute this fall."

Tiffany nodded and looked at Aiden. Her breath caught as he winked at her with his adorable smile twitching at the corners of his luscious mouth. The sight of those deep brown eyes caused her pulse to race. A sigh formed on her lips. How could she let the man she loved go, yet again?

Chapter 3

Aiden

Aiden drew up to the curb and cut the engine. All too soon his time with Tiffany was over.

"I wish you didn't have to go." Tiffany squeezed his hand. "I'll miss you."

Aiden bowed his head and exhaled a long slow breath. "The invitation is open." As he lifted his gaze to examine her sad face, his heart sank. "I'll visit when I have a free weekend."

Her eyes pleaded for his understanding. "I'm moving into the dorms, so my parents won't know if I go away for the weekend."

"That's perfect. I hope it's soon." He leaned toward her, cupping her cheek in his palm. "I love you."

She stared at him with shiny eyes. "I love you."

Aiden tipped his head and captured her lips, savoring her soft mouth and wished he didn't have to leave for Philly tomorrow.

"Aiden?" Tiffany blinked at him, playing with the hair at the nape of his neck. "You're leaving, so I have to ask. Are we exclusive?"

He frowned and lowered his hand. "What?"

"While you were gone, we weren't and—"

Aiden pressed a fingertip against her lips. "I'm willing, Tiff. Are you?"

She nodded. "I needed to make sure. You're moving so far away, and I don't know how often we'll see each other."

"If you want us to be together, we'll find a way."

She nodded and slid closer to kiss him deeply. "I'd better go inside, and you should go home and sleep. It's a long drive to Philadelphia."

Aiden wrapped her in his arms.

"I love you, Aiden." Tiffany pressed her lips to his one last time before she slipped from the car and dashed across the lawn. She glanced over her shoulder one final time before disappearing into the house.

And that was it. Tomorrow he'd be hundreds of miles away, which seemed as far away as being banished overseas.

Aiden surveyed the stack of boxes containing his books and personal items. Why his grandmother had rented this huge furnished apartment, he didn't know, but he wouldn't complain. It contained everything from high-end appliances right down to the cutlery. The location was amazing, being a scant five-minute walk from the medical school.

According to his information package, the complex had a full gym, a resident lounge with games and a pool table, and an expansive rooftop patio for the use of the residents, along with a swimming pool.

Not that he'd have much free time but hanging out on a sunny patio while he studied had a certain appeal.

He opened the fridge and freezer and grinned. The housekeeper had outdone herself.

It seemed out of character for his grandparents to be so generous in ensuring his comfort, but he supposed they were grateful he wasn't underfoot at their house. Or maybe his grandmother had acted alone, hoping to assuage her guilt.

After brewing coffee and eating a light breakfast, he unpacked the few items he'd brought in his car and hung his clothing. Once he completed the tasks, he scrolled through the contacts on his phone. "Will. Are you here?"

"I got in this morning." His friend's muffled yawn carried down the line.

"Let's grab a beer."

"I wish. They messed up my rental request, so I'm searching for a place to live. There's no affordable housing available, and I have zero furniture. Looks like a hostel for me."

"If you're interested, you could move into my extra bedroom."

"No way."

"We'd have to find you a bed, but otherwise the apartment is furnished."

"How much is the rent?"

"Good question." Aiden frowned. "My grandmother pays it. So, no rent."

Silence reigned for a moment.

"You're offering me a free room?"

"The rent's the same whether someone sleeps in the extra bedroom or not. You could use some of what you're saving to furnish your bedroom, but other than that—"

"Sold. Let me catch a cab. I have too much stuff to carry."

"I'll come to get you. Give me the address."

Aiden arrived less than twenty minutes later. Will waved from his perch on a pile of boxes as he sipped from a take-out cup.

"Whoa." His friend's eyebrows rose. "Who'd you steal that Beamer from?"

"Ha, funny guy. It's a belated birthday gift from my grandparents." Aiden popped the trunk. "All the better to get me out of town with."

They stowed Will's belongings and drove toward Aiden's apartment. It wasn't long before they turned onto his street.

"Nice." Will grinned as the door to the underground parking slid open. "How is it we spent so much time traveling together, and I never clued in you were Ritchie Rich?"

Aiden shrugged as he parked.

Will shot him a curious look and his brows rose. "You hate talking about your family, don't you?"

"There isn't much to say. Grab your suitcase, and I'll show you the apartment."

Will studied him on the way up to their floor, but his friend didn't push him to divulge any further information.

Aiden unlocked the door and ushered Will inside.

"This place is amazing." He followed Aiden upstairs and down the hallway to the extra bedroom. "Far cry from the minuscule cabin we shared on that sailboat, or some of the sketchy places we stayed during our travels."

"It sure is. I'm glad to help, and it'll be damn convenient for our study sessions. Even better, my grandmother arranged maid service, grocery delivery, and laundry."

"No laundromat or cleaning and a constant supply of food. You're a lifesaver."

"You might have to put up with my girlfriend visiting from Chicago."

"Girlfriend?" Will's eyebrows rose. "You've been home for a week."

"Long story, but we dated before I went overseas. Her name is Tiffany."

Will smirked. "Well, well. Aren't we the secretive one. I look forward to meeting the lovely lady soon."

"Maybe next weekend. We'll see." Aiden tossed Will the extra set of keys. "Now, let's buy you some furniture."

Aiden focused on the arrival gate. The constant stream of people signaled another flight had disembarked.

"Aiden." Tiffany's face lit up as she appeared with small carry-on bag in tow.

His heart lifted as he soaked up her bright, beautiful smile. He swept her from her feet, swinging her around and planting a long kiss onto her lips. "I've missed you."

"It's so good to see you. This week dragged by." She cupped his face between her hands, kissing him one more time. "Let's get out of here."

Aiden grabbed her bag in one hand, linking the fingers of the other with hers. After stowing her luggage in the trunk, he opened her door and settled her into the seat. "Hungry?"

She reached over to brush a stray hair from his forehead. "Not hungry … exactly."

"My place?" A grin spread across his face.

Her smile and nod were all the answer he needed.

The minute they walked in the door, he pulled her in for a kiss, and then led her upstairs to his room, closing the door behind them.

"This is beautiful."

"And so are you," he whispered against her hair as he wrapped her into an embrace from behind.

Tiffany turned and slid her arms around his neck. "Sweet talk will get you everywhere."

"Everywhere?" He raised a brow, before leaning in to capture her lips.

"Where's your roommate?"

"Out. It's Friday night. And he thought he'd give us some privacy since I haven't seen you in two weeks. How did you get away?"

"I told my mom I was busy with a school project, but I made it. Thank you for paying for my flight."

"Sorry you had to lie, but if they knew …"

"It's okay, Aiden." Tiffany peered up at him. "They've kept us apart for far too long. Let's make up for lost time."

The next morning, Aiden awoke with a smile as he remembered the night before. He rolled, brushing a hand over her hip as her sleepy blue eyes opened.

"I thought I was dreaming." A slow smile spread across her face.

"Nope. It's all real." He leaned in to kiss her luscious lips, sighing in contentment.

"I could get used to this. This place is amazing. I share a tiny dorm room with a girl named Hazel." Tiffany stretched and turned onto her back. "At least you know your roommate. And you have a private bedroom and bathroom. Hazel and I share both."

He stroked her hair. "You escaped living at home."

"But you can't stay with me when you visit." She tucked a stray wisp behind her ear. "We have single beds only five feet apart. It's worse than a convent. My parents outright refused to let me have an apartment."

"So, you don't have a signal? Like the old sock on the door?"

Tiffany laughed. "She'd love being banned from our room while we …" She wiggled her brows.

"Ah." He waved a hand. "I'll rent a hotel room so we can spend the entire weekend in bed and pig out on room service."

"You're not worried your grandparents will find out?"

"What if they do? I'm eighteen, and your birthday is less than two weeks away."

"I need my dad to pay my tuition. It's safer if I come here." She slid out of bed and pulled on one of his large t-shirts. "I need coffee."

"Done." He yanked on his jeans and followed as she swayed into the hallway and down the stairs, one slow step at a time. Aiden couldn't take his eyes off of her.

"Hey." Will looked up from his spot at the counter, his eyes widening at the sight of Tiffany. He threw a look at Aiden, a smirk twitching his lips. "I'm Will Kavanagh."

"Tiffany Baxter." She smiled at him before skirting into the kitchen and digging in the cabinet to retrieve a cup.

"Wow," Will mouthed, his gaze traveling over the blonde in the kitchen.

Aiden narrowed his eyes at his friend, cocking his head.

Will shrugged and bowed over his textbook, peeking up now and again as she searched the fridge for the cream. The t-shirt rode up, exposing her long shapely legs as she stretched to reach a glass for some orange juice.

Aiden joined Tiffany in the kitchen, leaning in to kiss her luscious lips and tug the shirt down. He couldn't blame his roommate for looking, even if she wasn't Will's usual type. The t-shirt fell above mid-thigh, and her hair cascaded in wild, tangled ringlets down her back. And when she smiled, his breath caught in his chest. Even first thing in the morning without an ounce of make-up, she looked stunning.

A mischievous sparkle appeared in her big blue eyes as she held out her arms. She graced him with a radiant smile as he lifted her onto the counter. "Thanks, sweetie." Tiffany planted a kiss on his lips, before inspecting the apartment from her perch. "Aiden. What's that?" She pointed.

"It's an early birthday present."

Tiffany's face lit up as she leaped down from the counter and bounced across the floor. She ran a fingertip over the large satin bow wrapped around the art table. "You did this for me?"

"Do you like it?" He set his cup on the counter in time to catch her as she launched herself into his arms. Aiden scooped her up, and she wrapped her bare legs around his waist.

"Are you kidding?" She gave him a long, passionate kiss. "That's amazing."

"I hope you'll visit often, and now you can work on your art while you're here."

Her bright smile lightened his heart. "I love it. Thank you." She snuggled against his chest. "Now I can visit every weekend."

He'd feared them being apart and had lost hope when she'd refused to move. Now it seemed she wanted to be here. With him. For now, if that was all she could offer, he'd take it.

Chapter 4

Tiffany

By Monday morning, Tiffany had returned to Chicago and her tiny crowded dorm room.

"You'll be late for class." Hazel's cheery voice carried through the bathroom door.

Tiffany padded into their shared room, rubbing her eyes. "Let me wake up."

"We'll pick up coffee on the way." Her roommate pulled a sweatshirt over her head. "What time did you get in last night?"

"Midnight?" Tiffany scrunched her nose, trying to remember the exact time that she'd tiptoed into the dorms. They'd booked her return trip as late as possible in order to draw out every precious moment together. She tugged on a pair of fresh jeans and a sweater, her mind traveling to those last moments before she hurried through the security queue and onto her plane. The hot, passionate never-ending kiss he'd bestowed on her. The ache lingered in her body for hours after they parted.

"Given the look on your face"—Hazel snickered—"this guy must be special."

"He is." Tiffany smiled at her reflection as she brushed her hair. She loved Aiden more now than she had when they were fifteen, even if it didn't seem possible.

"Why are you living in Chicago?"

"It's a long, complicated story." Tiffany shrugged.

"Why?"

"Our families aren't thrilled about our relationship. My father doesn't want me to see him."

"Isn't Aiden in medical school?" Hazel quirked a brow. "Who wouldn't want their daughter to date a doctor? And," the girl said, motioning to the frame beside Tiffany's bed, "he's scorching hot." Her roommate blushed. "Sorry for ogling your boyfriend, but damn."

Tiffany giggled, the heat rising in her face as she surveyed the photo taken at the beach on the last day of summer. "He's even better in person, so don't apologize. He's from a good family, he treats me like a princess, and I adore him. But we have to sneak around."

"Wow."

"If my dad finds out, he'll refuse to pay tuition. It's not ideal, but what other choice do I have? It'll take Aiden four years to finish medical school. So, we're making the best of it."

"I understand," Hazel said as she slung her pack over her shoulder. "If there's anything I can ever do to help, let me know."

"Thanks." Tiffany collected her bag and followed her roommate into the hallway, trailing her toward the stairs. Having the girl's support made her feel a little better, with her own friends all so far away.

The rest of September swept by, punctuated only by a stilted dinner to celebrate her eighteenth birthday with her parents at an upscale restaurant. She dug in at school, thankful Hazel had made good on her promise, texting her and sending pictures of the assignments from the weekend sessions she missed due to her frequent trips to Philly.

By the end of October, Tiffany had spent practically every weekend in Philly. Sometimes, she'd work at her art table while several of Aiden's classmates gathered around the table for a study session. Other times, she found herself alone, but only for a few hours at a stretch. The quiet times she soaked up the peace and absorbed herself in her own projects

Today being Friday, her immediate plan was to get to the airport. An impromptu quiz had caused her class to run late, and now Tiffany worried she'd miss her flight.

She charged down the hallway toward her dorm room, head down as she searched her bag for her key.

"About time you showed up." The gruff voice halted her in her tracks.

"What are you doing here?" Her eyes widened.

"We haven't seen you for weeks," her father said. "Pack a bag and I'll drive you home for the weekend."

"Oh, umm. I can't. I have a project due. After I drop off my things and change, I'm on my way to the studio."

"Bring it with you."

"It's a group project. We need access to the materials here." The smooth lie leaving her lips caused a twinge in her belly.

Her father crossed his arms. "Your mother will be disappointed, young lady. You've barely shown your face since you started school. And you turned down the spa weekend."

"I'm sorry." She twisted a lock of her hair around her finger, tugging at it as she stared at the floor. "I'll come out one day next week for dinner."

"Call your mother."

She turned her key in her fingers, reluctant to open the door. The image of her overnight bag, packed and sitting in plain sight on her bed, flitted through her mind.

David wagged a finger. "I expect you to be home for Thanksgiving next weekend."

She nodded even as her heart sank at the thought of missing even a single weekend cozied up with Aiden at his apartment.

"See that you're there." David spun and marched away.

Tiffany glanced over her shoulder, fiddling with the lock as he disappeared into the elevator, the doors sliding shut behind him. She dashed in, changed, and grabbed her overnight bag. Five minutes later, she was hurrying toward the transit station. Panic rose as she glanced at her watch, but she emitted a sigh of relief as an airport-bound train arrived two minutes later. It would be tight, but she should make it.

When she reached the airport, she claimed her boarding pass and joined the security line, boarding her flight with only moments to spare.

―⤏

In the late afternoon on the day before Thanksgiving, Tiffany slipped through the front door of her childhood home. The savory smells drifting through the air made her smile. Despite being forced to spend a precious long weekend here, she hid her excitement. Many of her friends had returned to Chicago for the weekend, including Aiden.

His grandmother had insisted he fly home for the holiday. Until now, he'd pleaded his heavy course load as an excuse to avoid visiting, but this time he'd agreed, knowing Tiffany, along with their group of closest friends, would be nearby.

After dropping her bag in her room, she wandered into the kitchen.

Her mother glanced up from her task of tossing apple slices with sugar and cinnamon in a large mixing bowl. "The prodigal daughter returns. You'd think you'd moved to another city." Her mother's gaze lifted briefly before she arranged the apples in the pie crust.

"School's been crazy busy."

"Every weekend?"

"We have projects due all the time." Tiffany slid onto a stool and reached across to snag one of the sugar-coated apple slices. She popped it into her mouth, savoring the sweet cinnamon-infused combination, half expecting her mother to slap her hand.

Michelle heaved out a sigh. "You know what's even more disappointing than never seeing my daughter?"

"What?"

"When she lies to my face."

A shiver ran through Tiffany's body, and her palms grew clammy.

"How's Aiden?"

"How would I know?" Tiffany mumbled, swiping her damp hands across her thighs.

"You've flown to Philadelphia every single weekend, and you haven't seen your boyfriend?"

"How do …?" She swallowed hard.

"You can't see that boy." Michelle crossed her arms. "You know your father's feelings on the matter."

Tears brimmed her eyes. "I love him."

"You think you do, but honey, you're far too young." Her mother grasped one hand and gave it a gentle squeeze. "We thought you were done with that foolishness. You can't run off to Philadelphia again, or your father will move you home."

"Why? I'm eighteen."

"Do you think he'll continue paying your tuition if you insist on seeing Aiden? Break it off. This weekend you'll stay home with your family."

"But Alex and Jenna will be home from school."

"Tiffany." Her mother took both of her hands and peered into her eyes. "Please, do this for me? If your dad gets involved it'll be much worse… for everyone. The relationship with Aiden can't go anywhere."

Tiffany yanked her hands away and brushed at her eyes. "Why is he so against Aiden? Why can't either of you understand that we love each other?" She stumbled out of the kitchen and dashed up the stairs to her room, slamming the door. Now they knew. It was over.

Tiffany hugged her pillow and remained curled up on her bed. True to their word, her parents had monopolized her time and kept her in their sights.

They'd confiscated her phone so she couldn't even call anyone. In return, she'd maintained a stony silence and barely eaten three bites of her dinner. Her mother had eyed her with concern and made her usual comment: *You're wasting away, Tiffany. You need to eat.*

Her father had said nothing about her not eating or about Aiden, pretending everything was normal. But he knew; she could tell from the occasional scathing look sent her way from under his dark, furrowed brows.

At the tap on her window, she slid from under the covers and tiptoed across the room. She opened the window several inches, shivering at the blast of chilly November air. "You can't be here," she whispered. "They know."

He nodded, rubbing her bare arm. "My car isn't far. We need to talk."

"Give me a minute." She shooed him away. As risky as it was, this might be their last opportunity for a while. Now that her parents knew, what would be the consequences if they discovered her sneaking out? After a moment of hesitation, she crept to her closet and located a heavy sweatshirt, tugging it over her head before arranging her pillows under her covers. With any luck, they'd assume she was sleeping.

She slid through the window and used her fingertips to pull it closed before picking her way down the trellis. The moment her feet touched the ground, he grasped her hand and tugged her toward the sidewalk. Soon, they were settled in his car and leaving her neighborhood.

"Now what?" Tiffany closed her eyes and bowed her head.

"I don't know," Aiden said. "But my grandparents know. I heard all about it."

Tiffany clenched her hands in her lap, the tears burning her eyes as the lyrics of *Truly, Madly, Deeply* taunted her from the stereo system. She peered up and spotted the familiar pillars and iron gates as the car slowed. "What are you doing?"

"Duck down." Aiden turned into the driveway of the mansion. "My grandparents are out at some stupid party."

Tiffany slid down in her seat until the overhead garage door closed.

Aiden opened the door and peeked into the hall, beckoning her to follow him up the service stairway to the second floor. Moments later, they were in his room with the door closed and locked behind them. He opened his arms to her. "We'll work it out." He cuddled her against his chest as he rubbed her back.

Tiffany pressed her face into his shoulder. "I love you."

Aiden tangled his hands in her hair and kissed her as she slid her hands under his sweater, tugging it over his head.

Every time they were together, it amazed her how he'd changed. She ran her palms up his biceps, over his smooth firm chest, and across his six-pack before plucking at the button on his jeans. "You've been working out."

"It was all that manual labor on the sailboat. And the skiing and surfing, and…" He closed his eyes. "I vowed I'd never let anyone push me around, ever again. Now they can't."

Tiffany bowed her head, resting her forehead against him. "Don't, Aiden. Please? Can we not…?"

"Shh." He kissed her hair before tucking a finger under her chin. "We don't have to—"

Tiffany pressed her lips to his to forestall any further discussion. Instead, she peeled off her shirt and unzipped his jeans. She led him to the massive bed and stripped off her own pants before pushing him onto the mattress. "No more talk," she whispered.

His lips crushed against hers, and she sighed against his mouth. This man had the power to make her forget everything but him.

And now, after a long loving session in his king-sized bed, she sighed and snuggled closer, not wanting their time together to end.

Being in his arms was incredibly comforting. She'd gotten used to being in his bed during all those visits to Philly. Aiden was the only man she'd ever woken up with beside her, and he was the only one she ever wanted for the rest of her life.

"I've been thinking …" Aiden murmured against her hair.

"About what?" She trickled her fingers over his bare chest.

"I love you, Tiff. What if …?" He shut his eyes and dragged in a breath.

The rapid tattoo of his heart vibrated her fingertips. "What?" She propped herself on one elbow and stared at him.

Aiden cupped her face between his palms. "I can't stand the thought of being without you. We have to make it happen before they find a way to separate us." He sat and a determined expression appeared. "Marry me."

Tiffany's heart almost stopped beating. She couldn't breathe. *Did he just …?* Her mouth dropped open, but words wouldn't come.

"Tiff?" He brushed his thumbs over her cheeks, staring deep into her eyes. "Say something."

"I-I …." She inhaled, blinking hard to quell the tears. "Are you asking me?"

"Tiffany Gabrielle Baxter, will you marry me?"

"Yes." The tears flooded her eyes, and she graced him with a watery smile. But, it faded as questions bombarded her mind. "Wait. How can we?"

"You're eighteen." Aiden shrugged. "How can he stop you? We'll go somewhere amazing and get married."

"Elope?" She pressed her trembling fingertips to her lips. "What about my tuition and school?"

"I can afford tuition for both of us."

Tiffany's heart fluttered and she nodded. "Yes, I'll marry you."

Aiden slid his hand under his pillow, producing a velvet jeweler's box.

Tiffany's eyes widened. She froze in place as he snapped it open. "Oh, wow."

Aiden lifted her hand and removed the ring from the padding, slipping it onto her finger. "It looks amazing."

"It does." She turned her hand, entranced at the way the light played across the diamonds. "Where did you get this?"

"It's an heirloom from my mother's side of the family."

Tiffany stared at it. "How did you get it?"

"My grandmother left it for me in her will. I could buy you a different one."

"No." She shook her head. "It's gorgeous. I love it." Tiffany admired the intricate design on the band. She'd never imagined receiving a ring this beautiful. "I don't know what to say."

"Yes is all I needed to hear. My grandparents had a long and happy marriage. I hope it brings us luck."

"When and how are we going to do this?"

"You have a passport, right?"

Tiffany nodded.

"Can you get your hands on it without your parents noticing?"

"I know where it is."

"Perfect. We'll leave just before Christmas break. Pack for the tropics. Leave the details to me."

Tiffany giggled. "I pictured Italy."

"We don't have enough time to do Italy justice, but we'll go someday." Aiden tucked a strand of hair behind her ear. "We have the rest of our lives, Tiff. I promise."

Tiffany placed her palms against his face. "I love you so much, Aiden. We'll be together, forever. That's my promise to you." She leaned in and kissed him, her heart soaring at the thought of being his wife. Once they married, no one could keep them apart, ever again.

Chapter 5

Aiden

Aiden hoped his luck would hold as he slipped in through the garage. He'd managed to sneak Tiffany in and out of the house without anyone noticing.

His heart pounded. He couldn't fathom the upcoming changes in his life. She'd said yes. Visions of the perfect location floated through his mind. Somewhere he'd never been. Somewhere fresh and new. A place they could form their own unique and special memories to treasure as a couple.

Tiffany deserved the best. She'd make sacrifices to be his wife, and he never wanted her to regret leaving Chicago. She'd forfeit a big white wedding with her friends and family in attendance. She couldn't even wear the ring or tell her friends until after they married.

Their friends would be upset, but their first unbreakable vow to each other was complete secrecy. One misplaced word to the wrong person could have disastrous results for their future.

"Where have you been?"

Aiden stopped short. "Nowhere."

"It must have been somewhere." Gramma Grace folded her arms and narrowed her eyes. "Stay away from that girl."

He shook his head and dropped his gaze to study the tiles on the floor.

"Aiden." His grandmother's voice softened. "I know how you feel about Tiffany, but she's here and you're in Philadelphia. David won't allow you near her. Please. Let her go."

"I can't," he whispered. "Why is it impossible for everyone to understand? Why don't you all back off and let us live our lives?"

"It's not my decision." Grace stepped closer. "I don't say this often enough, but I love you. I've missed having you here. If you pursue her, I fear I'll lose you." She placed a hand on his arm. "Don't make me go through endless years of missing you from my life. You're my only grandchild. I simply can't."

"I can tell you missed me." He shook off her hand, retreating two steps. "That's why I wasn't welcome to return home for all those years." He dashed up the stairs and slammed his bedroom door behind him. After a few deep breaths, he flopped onto his bed and picked up Tiffany's pillow. The light scent of her clung to the pillowcase, and he held it to his chest. *How could I give her up?*

He pushed away his grandmother's words. She had no right to make demands. Pain squeezed his heart as he closed his eyes, memories dancing through his head. Once, she'd been his beloved Gramma Grace. A grandmother who'd welcomed him for holidays while his parents jetted off on tropical vacations. A grandmother who'd traveled with him and invited him to the beach house every summer. *But, also a grandmother who'd forsaken me. A grandmother who failed me when I needed her most. Time after time.*

Aiden had begged his grandmother to bring him home after the first year abroad, but she'd refused. Alone at fifteen on the opposite side of the world, he'd endured three-years worth of holidays without a family. He'd persevered and survived by traveling and pretending he wasn't devastated. A lonely day-to-day existence, endured in silence due to not only threats, but the desire to protect the vulnerable girl he'd been forced to leave behind.

Time to stop the constant interference in his life and face the ugly truth. He had to choose. Family? Or the woman he loved?

Aiden pocketed his keys, glancing at his watch as he stepped onto the sidewalk. It had taken forever to escape his grandfather's lecture and the inquisition about where he was going and with whom. It seemed clear his grandmother had ratted him out, yet again.

"Well, look who's in town." The burly florid-faced man blocked his path.

Aiden straightened and met the man's cold gaze. "Get out of my way." His heart pounded. He hoped Tiffany hadn't cracked and given up their secret.

"I only want to talk." David Baxter held up his hands, palms facing Aiden. "About what?"

David crossed his arms. "You've caused my daughter enough trouble. There will be no further visits to Philadelphia. Stay away."

"She's eighteen. You can't keep her locked up."

"Perhaps not, but things won't go well for either of you if you insist on pursuing this. Your last run-in with my associates is just the beginning."

"Are you threatening me?"

"Not at all." The man smirked. "But you'll leave her alone. You both have promising futures. Keep it that way." The man shoved past him.

Aiden let out his breath and glanced over his shoulder as the man disappeared around the corner. Threats and intimidation were the hallmarks of David Baxter's dealings with anyone, including his daughter. Though he wished he could react or retaliate, that would bring trouble for Tiffany. He couldn't risk it.

After taking a moment to collect his thoughts and paste on a neutral expression, he pushed through the door of the diner, scanning the room.

Tom waved from the booth toward the back where he sat with Ryan and Joel.

Aiden straightened and forced himself to stroll casually toward the table. *Act natural.* These guys knew him too well. Keeping the plan under wraps was essential.

"Look who it is." Ryan punched his shoulder as Aiden slid in beside him. "You're late. We were about to send a search party."

"I got waylaid." Aiden motioned at the waitress to fill his cup.

"Your grandfather?" Tom lifted an eyebrow.

Aiden shrugged as he added a touch of cream and sugar. "And David Baxter. I ran into him on the street just now."

"Oh-oh." Joel's brows lifted. "What's going on?"

"More orders to stay away from his daughter." Aiden sighed. "They know she's visited Philly, so the commandments of the high-and-mighty man himself have rained upon us." He rolled his eyes.

"Shit." Tom shook his head. "The two of you should cool it. It'll blow over."

"Yeah, maybe." Aiden rubbed a hand through his hair and avoided Tom's gaze. "So, Ryan. How's California?"

The Thanksgiving weekend had been endless. It was only Saturday, and he'd been forced into a formal suit complete with bow tie. His grandparents loved to entertain, and they expected Aiden to play his part as the dutiful grandson. By the end of dinner, he longed to escape the crowded, stuffy room, but it would be hours before the last of the Chicago elite were bundled into limos for their journey home.

"Hey." Tom appeared beside him.

"I didn't know you were coming."

"Since when does your grandfather have one of these parties without my grandfather making an appearance? Thought I'd tag along." Tom smirked, motioning to the crowd of over-dressed socialites with their middle-aged husbands. "They hope this will be us in a few years."

Aiden glanced around. "I damn sure hope not. If I end up like that…" He shuddered

"Boggles the mind," Tom whispered. "Let's get out of here."

They slipped out the door, trudging through the snow toward the pool house. Skirting around to the back, they stepped into the small entertainment room.

Aiden slid off his coat and cranked up the stereo system.

"Ah." Tom removed his jacket and tie before dropping onto the couch. He waved the joint pinched between his fingers.

"Bless you."

"No problem. I figured a little MJ was just what the doctor ordered." Tom snickered. "It'll take the edge off."

Aiden scoffed at the sad little pun. "I'm not one yet."

"Close enough." Tom produced a lighter and touched the flickering flame to the tip before taking a long drag. He offered it to Aiden.

Aiden inhaled, holding the smoke in his lungs for several moments. He leaned back and closed his eyes as he blew it out in a long steady stream.

They passed it back and forth in silence, listening to the heavy bass of the music thumping through the room.

"What's really going on?"

Aiden blinked before turning his head toward his long-time friend. "Huh?"

"I've known you all of your life, Aiden. Be careful. She's already taken out a chunk and we've only gotten you back."

"Should have seen this coming." He took another hit and then passed the joint back to Tom.

"Yup. Neither Joel or Ryan fell for your BS story. So, spill it."

"What can I say?" Aiden shrugged. "Our families, especially her father and my grandfather, are against our relationship. They demanded I stay away and informed me she won't be visiting Philly. Nothing more to say." He closed his eyes again, hoping Tom would drop it.

"But you won't stay away. You're plotting something. Don't do anything stupid." Tom straightened. "Aiden?"

"I hear you. I won't, okay?"

"You'd better not. Get your shit together and finish medical school. That man is poison and will stop at nothing to get his way. We both know it." Tom leaned back. "You're like my brother. The crap they've put you through pisses me off," he said.

Aiden shook his head and kept his eyes closed as lethargy stole over him. Some days he could barely deal with life and keep his head straight. Tom had been a rock through so many of the ups and downs, and he hated keeping secrets from the guy.

But, there was no alternative. He hoped his friend would forgive him when he learned the truth.

―

The next three weeks were exhausting. Keeping his focus became increasingly difficult as the days wore on. But now at least he had a game plan. The end of their separation was in sight.

The marker squeaked across the whiteboard as the professor's voice faded out. Keeping his attention on the lecture wasn't easy.

Aiden sorted through the plan again, searching for that loophole or tiny detail he'd missed. They'd only have one shot.

"Hey." His classmate, Matthias, smacked his arm. "You'll be late for our next class."

"Huh?" Aiden blinked.

The buzz of conversation and rustle of papers filled the room as everyone gathered their laptops and notebooks.

"You've been acting weird ever since you got back from Chicago. Everything okay?"

"Fine."

Will joined them as they headed toward the back of the room and exited into the hallway. "Tiffany hasn't been out for a couple of weeks now."

"Girl troubles." Matthias nodded. "My girlfriend in New Orleans is having issues with me being away at school. It's difficult. I won't see her again until Christmas."

"Tiffany's dad forbids her to come to Philly." Aiden sighed. "We've been apart for weeks."

Will grinned. "I wouldn't mind having her as a roommate."

"Hey." Aiden threw a dark look his way.

"Kidding, man. I'm kidding." Will held up his hands to fend off the light punch Aiden dealt him.

"Right." Aiden fought the twitching of his lips.

Though he felt guilty keeping the truth from his friends, it was a relief to know they'd accept Tiffany when she joined him in Philly. Only a few more days, and it would all come to fruition.

Chapter 6

Tiffany

December blew in along with a load of snow and frigid winds. Tiffany shivered as she yanked on her sweater and scooped her hair into a ponytail. She stared in the mirror, taking in the dark circles under her eyes and her pale face.

It had been weeks since she'd seen Aiden—not since Thanksgiving. The way things were going, she wouldn't see him anytime soon. Her dad had been monitoring her movements, so sneaking onto a plane would be impossible.

They'd both vowed to remain patient, but the days stretched before her endlessly. Would he pull it off and follow through with his promises?

She slung her pack over her shoulder, she shuffled down the hallway, taking her time to reach the classroom. She dropped into the seat beside her roommate.

"This is for you." Hazel shoved an envelope into her hand.

Tiffany stared at it for a second before breaking the seal. The words danced up at her. "How did you get this?"

"Some guy asked if I knew you, then gave me that."

Tiffany exhaled a long breath. "When?"

"Just before class. He seemed to know who I was."

"Aiden?" Tiffany shot a glance at Hazel.

"No. A messenger. From what you've said, your boyfriend wouldn't risk being seen. Would he?"

Tiffany shook her head. "Can you cover for me?" Her heart pounded as she thought about what she was about to do. "It's time for plan B."

Hazel grinned. "This is exciting. Like a love story in a movie. Reuniting the star-crossed lovers."

Tiffany almost laughed, except for the fact that it wasn't funny. Hazel's comment hit the mark. The course of their relationship had been a series of rough battles and stormy seas. A happily-ever-after ending would be a miracle.

For the remainder of the day, Tiffany continuously surveyed her surroundings. She wouldn't put it past her father to have her under surveillance. He seemed determined to keep her from Aiden.

"Stop that," Hazel whispered. "If someone is watching, then they'll know something is up. Play it cool. It'll be fine."

She forced herself to keep her eyes focused toward the front of the room. Have patience, she reminded herself. If she kept it together, she'd soon be reunited with Aiden.

As the week crawled by, Tiffany spent most of her time making the necessary arrangements. Over Thanksgiving, she'd managed to locate her passport, collect clothing from her room, and she'd added a few new items to her wardrobe, preparing herself for a swift exit.

"Wish me luck." Tiffany donned the dark wig Hazel had purchased for her.

Hazel hugged her, rubbing her back. "Remember, stay calm and cool."

Tiffany nodded before stepping from her dorm room, dragging her suitcase. She forced herself to keep an even and unhurried pace as she began her journey. Every step down the hallway counted as one step closer to Aiden.

Before she exited onto the street, she wrapped the borrowed scarf around her face, not only to block the howling wind, but also to hide her features. She strode toward the station with assurance and purpose, keeping her eyes focused straight ahead. As Hazel had reminded, the more she panicked she looked, the more attention she drew. The key to avoiding detection was blending in.

Once on the train, she sank into a seat and stared at the grimy floor until they left the station. Only then did she lift her head and contemplate her reflection in the window. With her roommate's gray wool coat and the mousy brown wig, she barely recognized herself.

At the airport, she ducked into the bathroom and disposed of the wig in the trashcan. After tucking her scarf into her bag, slung the coat over her arm, and proceeded through the terminal to join the line for check-in.

"Thank you." She accepted her boarding pass from the agent and sent her bag down the conveyor. *Almost there.* After a calming breath, she proceeded to the security queue, focusing on adding her belongings to the gray bin. Within a few minutes, she'd cleared the scanners and headed to the departure gate.

Aiden's face lit up as he spotted her. "You made it." He embraced her.

"Fortunately." Tears threatened to overwhelm her, but her stomach had settled considerably now that she was in his arms. "I kept waiting for my father to appear and drag me back to school."

"We've been careful. Our boarding call should be announced soon." He rubbed her back. "Stay calm, we're almost there."

They located two empty seats and she clutched his hand, focusing on the woman in the row of chairs across the aisle. A little blonde girl, maybe four years old, snuggled against her mother's chest with her arms around the woman's neck.

The sob escaped without warning, and Aiden's grip on her hand tightened. Tiffany tore her gaze away, blinking hard as the burn of tears intensified.

He slipped an arm around her. "We don't have to do this."

"I want to," she whispered.

Moments later, the first class boarding announcement echoed through the terminal, and Aiden rose, pulling her to her feet. "Ready?"

The urge to glance over her shoulder was hard to resist, but she clung to his hand and concentrated on reaching the end of the jetway. As the flight attendant ushered them into their row, she issued a sigh of relief and busied herself by settling into her wide plush seat.

"Relax," he muttered as he linked their fingers. "Five minutes, and we'll be out of here."

She nodded. "I'm okay. Hazel covered for me."

"Bless that girl. We'll have to buy her a thank you gift."

Tiffany exhaled a long slow breath at the familiar clunk of the door closing and locking, followed by a tiny jolt as the airplane was pushed away from the gate and began its tedious journey toward the runway.

At last, the engines roared and they sped forward, a familiar sense of weightlessness taking over for a split second as the jet lifted from the ground, punctuated moments later by the clunk of the wheel mechanism retracting underneath the airliner.

"We did it." She heaved out a sigh, flooded with relief.

"Yeah, we did." Aiden brushed her hair back, tucking it behind her ear before leaning in to kiss her. "I love you, Tiff." Aiden reached into his pocket, produced the familiar velvet box, and popped it open.

Tiffany extended her hand, allowing him to slip the magnificent ring onto her finger. "And I love you."

A smile crept over Tiffany's face at her newly minted memories. She was in Aruba. On her honeymoon. With the love of her life. His bare body nestled against hers. The soft wisps of his breath tickled her neck, proving it wasn't just a fantastic dream. "Wake up." She shook him. "Aiden."

"Morning, beautiful." His hand skimmed over her hip before he pulled her closer.

Tiffany giggled as he nuzzled against her neck. "Stop … stop." She burst into laughter. "It tickles."

Aiden hovered over her, dropping tender kisses on her neck. "I love you, Tiff."

"I love you, my handsome husband." She batted her eyes at him. "That's surreal. I have a husband."

"And don't you forget it." Aiden entwined their left hands, kissing each of her fingers in turn. "Do you like your rings?"

Tiffany gazed at the heirloom with its glittering diamonds. "They're gorgeous and incredibly special. Won't your grandparents freak out when they find out about the ring?"

"At us getting married? Absolutely. But these rings are from my mother's side of the family, so any freaking out would be unwarranted." He propped himself up on one elbow. "They were married for sixty-five years, and they were happy. That would be amazing."

"We'll be married forever. This whole thing has been incredible." She brushed her fingertips across his cheek. "I have something for you. I'm sorry it couldn't be more, but …" She retrieved the envelope from under her pillow.

Aiden kneeled on the bed, breaking the seal. A slow grin spread across his face. "Wow, Tiffany. This is incredible. You drew this?" He traced a fingertip over the intricate design.

"You've always wanted a tattoo, and this suits you." She shrugged.

"I love it. When we get home, we'll visit Chicago."

"Yes. Can you imagine? That artist will do justice to my design." She bounced in excitement. "She's the best in town." She smiled and pulled out another envelope and revealed the picture inside.

"No way. You're getting one?"

"If I don't chicken out. What if it hurts?"

"I'll hold your hand. It'll look amazing."

"You like it?" Tiffany had spent countless hours designing and perfecting the templates. It meant everything to see Aiden excited about permanently displaying it on his body.

"It's perfect. Thank you." He rewarded her by capturing her lips in a heart-stopping kiss.

"Mmm." She sighed as she caressed his cheek. "I wanted to buy you something, but I couldn't afford it."

"This is more special than anything you could have found in a store. The hours you must have put into these. Wow. It's exactly what I wanted. Thank you." Aiden kissed her again, smoothing back her hair.

"My first official commission is a success." She grinned.

"It sure is. Where should I put it?" He studied the tattoo, tapping his index finger against his lips.

"Right here." Tiffany grazed her fingertips over his shoulder, loving how he twitched under the light stroke of her touch. "I pictured where it would go while I drew it." She traced the outline of the tattoo on his warm smooth skin, closing her eyes and imagining how it would look.

"Where are we putting yours?"

"Here." She slid her fingers a touch lower, moving toward the center of his back. "That way I can show it off whenever I want, but I can also hide it for work."

"You're an artist. Does it matter if someone sees it?"

"I want to own a gallery. Women have a tough enough time being taken seriously in the business world. A visible tattoo will give the wrong impression."

"On you, it will look sexy."

"I have the best husband in the entire world," she whispered as she stared into his eyes. "I will always love you, Aiden Hamilton." She smiled and twirled the ring on his finger.

"I love you, Tiffany Gabrielle Hamilton."

Tiffany stretched out on the lounger and adjusted her sunglasses. The palm trees swayed in the breeze as the sun kissed her skin. Never had she been so happy. Every single day had been magical and spent enjoying the sun and surf, but mostly, she enjoyed waking up in the security of her husband's arms.

Tomorrow the dream would be over. She had no idea what the reaction and subsequent fallout would be upon their return, or if their presence had even been missed.

If they had been missed and anyone thought to check their passports, it would be easy enough to locate them, but the remaining plans had been carefully executed. Though he had unfettered access to his family's travel account, Aiden had chosen to obtain a brand new credit card along with a travel agent in Philadelphia to plan their escape.

"What are you thinking?" Aiden squeezed her hand.

"I don't want to go home. I wish we could stay here forever, just you and me."

"I know what you mean." He closed his eyes, keeping tight hold of her hand.

"We have to face our families," she whispered. "My parents will freak. I don't know ..." Visions of being pulled into the office and berated endlessly flew through her mind.

"Hey." Aiden wiggled over, pulling her to join him on his lounge chair. "Why so worried? Did we do the wrong thing?"

"No, we did the exact right thing, but my father won't be happy." She snuggled into his waiting arms.

"Don't you worry about him. This time, you don't have to face anyone alone."

Chapter 7

Aiden

Despite the assurances he'd given Tiffany on their last night in Aruba, Aiden's heart pounded as they touched down in Chicago. He'd been tempted to go straight to Philadelphia and avoid the issue, but that solved nothing. Their families would either accept their marriage and support them or turn away and cut them both off. Rather than running away like a coward, he chose to face it head-on.

"We're home." Tiffany's tremulous voice cut into his thoughts.

"It'll be okay, Tiff." Aiden squeezed her hand before wrangling their carry-on bag from the overhead bin. Tucking her hand into his, he led her from the plane.

Her grateful smile warmed his heart. "I love you." She clung to him for the entire walk to the baggage carousel.

Nobody greeted them as they claimed their bags, but he hadn't expected a reception. Instead, he texted the long-term parking lot with his tag number and they boarded a shuttle.

"You drove?" Tiffany raised a brow as she spotted his car waiting by the steel chain-link gates.

"We need to pack your dorm and reclaim some belongings from your room at home. And it was easier to fly under the radar that way." Aiden shrugged. "I don't know how this will go with either of our families."

"My prediction is not great." Tiffany fidgeted with her wedding band as they pulled into traffic. "We should head to my house now. My dad won't be home, so I can pack before the massive blowout."

"Good idea. I don't have the same issues. My stuff is in Philadelphia."

She rolled her eyes at him. "Like you wouldn't avoid seeing your grandfather if you could?"

"Maaaaaybe." He tapped his fingers on the steering wheel. "We can go to your dorm room last."

It wasn't long before Aiden parked at the side of the driveway in front of her parents' house.

"Mom?" Tiffany peered down the hallway as they stepped into the foyer. Silence greeted them. "They aren't home." She cast a wide-eyed glance his way.

"Let's get what you need into the car." Aiden followed her as she dashed up the stairs.

She pulled her extra suitcases from the closet and began piling the remainder of her clothes into it.

"I'll do that. You check your bathroom and clear out any other personal items you want." He glanced around. "Pretty bare in here."

"I packed a bunch of boxes and moved them into storage during the Thanksgiving weekend and hid them at the back of the attic." She shrugged. "I didn't have much else to do as they wouldn't let me go out."

Aiden nodded as she cleared her dresser and side tables. Once the suitcases were full, he lugged them outside and stowed them in his trunk.

"Now what?" Tiffany fidgeted and straightened the rings on her left hand. "I don't even know if I want to see them."

"Too late to avoid that now." He motioned his head toward the sleek black car turning into the driveway. "At least talk to your mom." Michelle Baxter had always been kind to him, even as a teenage boy. Though that was before … In more recent history, she seemed to be no more than David's pawn.

Her mother emerged from her car, scurrying toward them. "Tiffany. Where have you been? I've been trying to phone you for days." Michelle pulled her daughter into a hug. She peered over Tiffany's shoulder toward Aiden and frowned. "You should go before David gets home. He's livid."

"I'm not leaving without Tiffany." He gazed at the woman steadily, refusing to blink.

Michelle held her daughter by the shoulders. "You look so tanned. Where have you been?"

"We went to Aruba." Tiffany's voice shook. "We got married." She held up her left hand.

"No." Michelle grabbed her daughter's fingers. "Oh, honey." Tears flooded her mother's eyes.

"I love him, Mom. It's the only way we can be together. I'm moving to Philadelphia."

Her mother brushed at her damp cheeks. "You got married, and I missed it," she whispered. A furrow appeared on her brow and she covered the few paces to Aiden.

His breath caught and he tensed, ready for the onslaught, but he forced himself to hold his ground.

Michelle embraced him. "You take good care of my girl. Things are about to get crazy, so you two should leave while you can."

"I love her," he whispered as he hugged her back. "I'll make sure she's okay, always."

Tiffany sniffled, and then dashed to the car, hauling out two packages. "I bought you presents for Christmas."

"Wait. I have something for you too." Michelle hauled her daughter toward the house.

They followed, Aiden slipping an arm around Tiffany as her mother disappeared inside.

"Here. Your gifts." Michelle shoved them into her daughter's hands. "Now go." She guided Tiffany toward the front door.

"Bye, Mom." Tiffany turned away. Tears glistened on her cheek as he settled her in the passenger seat.

A small sob broke free from the woman beside him as they backed out of the driveway. She clenched one of the parcels between her hands in her lap, tugging at the ribbon. Her gaze seemed fixed on the closed front door.

Aiden clenched his jaw, noting that Michelle had retreated into the safety of her house, not even bothering to wave goodbye. Once they were several blocks away, he pulled to the curb. "Are you okay?"

"No." Tiffany shook her head. "She barely reacted and sent me away. Just like ..." She burst into tears.

"Honey." Aiden pulled her to his chest, rocking gently.

This wasn't turning out at all as he'd hoped. He'd expected anger, but Michelle's reaction confused him. An ache formed in his heart. The one person he hoped would be their ally had pushed them away.

Only twenty minutes later, they drove through the massive gates at his grandparents' home.

"Are you sure you want to do this now?" he asked.

She turned her pale face his way, dabbing at her puffy red-rimmed eyes. "Let's get it over with. I'm ready to go home."

Aiden led her into the silent house. There was no dash up the stairs this time. The few items he owned had been moved to Philadelphia months ago.

"Aiden?" His grandmother stepped from the library, her gaze scanning over the two of them as she approached. "I wondered when you'd reappear. Your grandfather is extremely unhappy."

He quelled the snort that wanted to erupt. His grandfather was never happy. "Grandmother." He kissed her cheek. "Where is he?"

"At the office." She sighed. "You'd best come in." Beckoning them, she retraced her steps to the large wood-paneled room. The fire dancing merrily on the hearth belied the somber atmosphere.

Aiden sat on the overstuffed sofa, pulling Tiffany down beside him. He waited while his grandmother settled into her usual chair.

"You'd best tell me what you did."

Aiden cleared his throat. "You haven't guessed?"

"I suspected when David Baxter barged in here all upset. Then of course, we couldn't reach you on the phone and learned you'd both left school early." Grace's keen eyes rested on Tiffany's hand. "You gave her the rings."

"Yes."

His grandmother studied them for an interminably long time. "They look lovely on you, dear. Have you told your parents?"

"We saw my mother. I'm sure she's called my father by now." Tiffany bowed her head. "She wasn't thrilled, and I'm sure you feel the same." She twined a finger into her hair, tugging at it. "We should go."

Aiden disentangled her hand from her blonde locks, bringing it to rest on his knee.

"I'll break the news to Thomas if David hasn't advised him. It would be wise to let things settle before he sees you." Grace folded her hands. "I do hope you'll be happy. Give me a moment. I have something to give you before you go."

Tiffany turned to him the moment his grandmother left the room. "Well, no shouting but …" She sighed.

Grace returned, stalling any attempt on his part to respond.

"I thought you should have your Christmas gifts. And this is for you." She handed a small velvet box to Tiffany. "It's a small wedding gift. I didn't get to see my only grandson married." His grandmother pressed a hand to her chest, her eyes becoming suspiciously shiny.

Another pang hit. Some shouting or a display of anger would have been preferable to this not-so-subtle guilt trip.

"Thank you." Tiffany accepted the box, looking up as Grace placed a hand over hers.

"Marriage is never easy, and you two are young. It will be even more difficult with so much stacked against you. Take care of each other."

Aiden rose and allowed her to hug him, and then stepped back as she embraced his new wife. *Wife.* How strange that sounded, even to his own ears.

A few minutes later, they were in the car, leaving the mansion for what felt like the last time. Aiden wondered yet again if they'd made the right decision. For him, it was nothing new. He'd survived many events and several years depending only on himself. And with any luck, the long-term friendships he'd formed would carry him through—or so he hoped.

Tiffany, however, appeared forlorn. As hard as her parents were to deal with, they were her only family. He hadn't expected warm best wishes or much support, but the reality of the situation sank in. Their actions would seem impulsive to some and might permanently sever the ties with their parents. Chances that they'd celebrate joyful Christmases or other holidays with their families was slim. He and Tiffany were on their own. He'd have to live with taking her away from what little family she had.

After they'd cleared her dorm room, Aiden checked them into a hotel suite, not wanting to attempt the long drive back to Philly. Exhaustion blurred his eyes, and all signs pointed to an imminent breakdown for his new wife.

The moment the door closed behind the bellman, Tiffany crawled onto the bed and curled into a ball, clutching a pillow to her chest. She hadn't bothered to explore the room or even peek out the window to admire the magnificent view.

Aiden joined her, wrapping himself around her. At this moment, there were no words. He couldn't ask if she was okay. Clearly, she wasn't. Instead, he held her close, taking comfort in the warmth of her body.

Tiffany entwined their fingers, brought his hands to her chest, and wiggled against him so there wasn't even the smallest bit of space between them. Gradually, her tense muscles relaxed, her grip loosened, and her breathing became soft and even.

Aiden didn't dare move, but he closed his eyes, drifting in his thoughts as she slept. Her joy had been stolen, but he'd find a way to make her happy.

"Aiden?" Warm fingertips caressed his skin. "Are you awake?"

He opened his eyes, blinking sleepily as he cupped her cheek with his hand. "Sleep well?"

"I was so tired," she whispered.

"Want to talk about it?"

"What is there to say? My mother took his side, as usual. And nobody insisted we stay for the holidays." A bitter tone crept into her voice. "Now we're orphans."

"I'm sorry," he said. "I didn't want it to end like this."

"It's not your fault. It's them. And you know what?" An icy fire erupted in her eyes. "Screw them. Every single damn one of them. I'm over it. They've treated me"—a broken sob issued from her throat—"like they own me. I refuse to live under their thumbs. Tomorrow, we'll go to our home to Philadelphia and put it, and them, behind us. It's time to start our life together."

"Sounds like a plan." Aiden pasted on a smile, recognizing that her anger covered the deep pain of rejection. He'd become far too familiar with the scenario himself, but if they became a solid unwavering unit, maybe they'd overcome it.

"If they want to force us to choose, then fine. I choose us." Her sweet warm breath wafted across his cheek. "I love you." Without waiting for a response, she pressed her lips to his, her soft hands sliding under his shirt, tugging it upward.

Aiden divested the offending article of clothing and helped her with her own. In moments, her fingers were working at the button on his jeans, and he tossed aside her lacy bra. Right now, she must hunger for warmth and closeness, and he understood. He longed for the same things.

―※―

The next morning, they left Chicago in the early hours to avoid the inevitable rush-hour traffic. Tiffany reclined her seat slightly, leaning back and closing her eyes. She reached across and rested her hand on the nape of his neck, her fingertips performing a delicate and gentle massage of his tense muscles.

"Did you open it?" he asked after they'd been on the road for an hour.

"Hmmm?" Her crystal-blue eyes turned his way.

"The gift from my grandmother." He met her gaze briefly before turning his attention to the slippery road. Flakes of snow drove into the windshield, making him hope it would stop soon. "What did she give you?" From the corner of his eye, he noted the half-shrug and the turn of her head toward the frosty glass of the passenger window.

Tiffany propped her chin on her balled fist, a heavy sigh issuing from her lips. "Why did she bother?"

For that, he had no answer. He clenched his hands around the steering wheel, wishing he could find the right words to ease her pain.

"I'm sorry," she whispered after several minutes.

Aiden gave his head a small shake and captured her hand, resting their entwined fingers on his thigh.

Hours later, when the light had faded and dusk settled in, they finally arrived in Philly. The apartment was dark and silent, and he found a note from Will, stating he'd returned home for the holidays. For Aiden, it seemed like the best possible scenario. They'd have the apartment to themselves for the entire holiday, giving them time to settle into married life.

"I'm exhausted." Tiffany rubbed at her eyes and smothered a wide yawn.

"Off to bed, then." He steered her toward the stairs. "I'll be up soon." The moment the door clicked shut behind her, he dug out his phone. The list showed numerous missed calls, all from the same number.

"What. The. Hell."

"Well, hello to you." Aiden brushed a hand through his hair as he dropped onto the couch.

"You promised not to do something stupid." Tom's deep voice boomed down the line. "Imagine my surprise when my grandfather asked if I knew you were planning to run off and *get married*."

"Sorry, but we had to—"

"Have you lost your mind? You married her? That's your definition of not doing anything stupid?"

Aiden's breath caught in his chest and disappointment flooded him. "I thought at least you would understand."

"You thought wrong. You've been back together for four entire months and you put a ring on her finger? Why? What the hell were you thinking?"

Aiden hit the disconnect button. The last thing he needed to hear was another person berating him for their choices.

His phone rang, but he held the shutdown button. Even his best friend in the world was against him, and he couldn't deal with it. Not at this moment, at any rate. He had enough contending with Tiffany's sadness.

"Hey, come to bed." Tiffany appeared, holding out her hand. "Are you okay?"

"Fine. It was a long drive is all." He linked their fingers and let her lead him to their bedroom.

Chapter 8

Tiffany

TIFFANY PLACED THE LAST GIFT under the tree and stepped back to admire the results. They'd spent the morning combing the tree lot, followed by a vest to the local craft market to purchase decorations and lights.

"Looks great." Aiden slid his arms around her waist from behind, cuddling her against him.

"Our first holiday as a married couple." She turned, stretching to kiss his warm lips.

"The first of many," he murmured before returning the kiss.

Tiffany rested her head against his chest and snuggled closer. At moments like these, it seemed as if everything would be okay. She appreciated that Aiden had made her feel welcome, and now she was comfortably settled into their home. He'd even paid for her art school tuition for the term starting in January.

"I have something for you." He offered her a small gift bag.

She peeked inside, pushing aside the red tissue paper. "Awww. This is cute." With a smile, she revealed the small ceramic gingerbread couple sharing a kiss under their own tree. *Aiden & Tiffany. Our first Christmas.* "You are such a romantic sap." Even as the words left her lips, emotion rushed through her and her chest tightened. "Thank you," she whispered as she found a spot to hang it.

"Perfect." He looped an arm around her waist.

"I love it." Her eyes burned. As illogical as it seemed, she missed her mother. They were often at odds in her recent memory, and her mother was often unapproachable and icy. Then Tiffany would picture her life as a young child and revisit the memories of hugs and kisses, infinite trips to the beach, and the night-time cuddling combined with a special bedtime story. These moments mixed with the reality of who her mother had become after her father had dived into the political arena. Michelle's former and current personas no longer jived, and for Tiffany, that was painful.

"What's the matter, sweetie?" Aiden dropped a kiss on her hair.

She shrugged and buried her head against his broad chest, unable to voice her feelings. Perhaps she didn't need to, because Aiden understood. He lived a similar reality with his own messed-up and politically motivated relatives.

"It'll get easier," he whispered. "I promise."

Tiffany peeked up at him. "How can you know?"

"It's the story of my life." His embraced tightened. "I haven't had a family Christmas since my parents moved to New York. For the past three years, I've been overseas and the year before that—"

"Please don't." She dropped her head and fought the rush of tears. "Let's not do that."

Aiden lifted her chin. "We have to talk about it sometime."

"No, we don't." She shook her head, trying to eliminate his words from her mind. "I put it all behind me, and I never, ever want to discuss it."

"But—"

"No!" Tiffany tore herself from his arms and dashed for the stairs. She threw herself onto their bed and curled into a ball. *Didn't he understand what I'd been through? What I had endured alone?*

Scalding tears flowed down her cheeks as her resentment blossomed. He knew nothing. During the years she'd spent confined in Chicago, he'd traveled overseas and experienced life. She would have loved to be away from the endless disappointment and lectures lavished on her by her family.

"I'm sorry."

Tiffany clutched her pillow and turned her head away.

The mattress sank as he lowered himself onto the bed and rubbed her back. After a long heavy sigh, he laid alongside her, moving close enough to wrap her in his arms. "We'll be okay, Tiff. I love you. And I'm sorry. I'm so, so sorry for everything that happened."

"Stop," she whispered. "I can't. Don't you understand? There's nothing to say."

They fell into a deep silence, but his presence and the heat of his body seeping into her back was of some comfort. He rested his cheek against her hair. The way his warm breath tickled her neck, his strong arms cradling her as he rubbed her arm soothed her.

Tiffany caressed his hand, unable to speak, but not wanting him to leave. She loved every single second this man gave her, his attention filling the void in her heart. Even given the difficulties they faced, she could manage if they were together.

~

"Hey." The door crashed against the wall as it was flung open. "Get up. We should—"

Tiffany bolted upright and yanked the sheet around her as she stared wide-eyed at Will.

"Oh." The man turned away, a flush rising in his face. "Sorry. I thought you were alone."

"What are you doing here?" Aiden sat and rubbed at his eyes.

"I live here?"

"I thought you were coming home tomorrow."

Tiffany reached for Aiden's oversized t-shirt and slid it over her head. "I'm decent."

Will peered at them and laughed. "Yeah, but he isn't."

She realized she'd claimed all the covers, leaving Aiden with only a wisp of the sheet draped over his naked body.

"Whatever." Aiden hauled the covers over himself. "Why'd you barge in?"

"I decided to come home early to get ready for New Year's and thought about grabbing a beer and playing some pool, but it appears you have company." He grinned. "Nice to see you again, Tiffany. You two work everything out with the families?"

"Not exactly." Aiden swept a hand through his hair.

Tiffany sidled into the bathroom and pushed the door closed with her foot.

"You what?" Will's voice carried through the door. His tone softened, and his words became indistinct murmurs.

She knew what they were discussing, but she only caught an occasional word. Not that she needed to hear what Will was saying. Aiden had valiantly hidden how upset he was about Tom's less-than-thrilled reaction, and it seemed Will was equally as excited about the news.

Aiden hadn't realized that she'd overheard the disappointing words spoken between him and his best friend the night they arrived in Philly. It had put a damper on things and darkened his mood over the holidays. It certainly hadn't been a dream Christmas. She mourned the loss of the little family she had, and Aiden pretended that things between him and his friends were fine.

Big fat liar. He'd avoided every incoming call, including those from Ryan and Joel, along with those from his friends here in Philly. *I want us to have a quiet first Christmas, just the two of us,* he'd said when she'd attempted to discuss the subject.

By the time she returned to the bedroom, Will was nowhere in sight. Aiden had his head buried in his pillow.

She padded across the room and crawled onto the bed. "Aiden?" Shaking his shoulder, she leaned over him. "What did he say?"

"Oh, he's thrilled," he muttered.

Tiffany propped herself against the headboard and drew her knees to her chest. She stared at the beautiful sparkling diamonds adorning her finger. Why couldn't anyone even pretend to be on their side?

Aiden rolled toward her. "Don't cry, please?" He gazed at her. "Tiff?" He sat and rubbed her arm.

Her chin trembled as she bit her lip. It seemed like all she had done recently was weep. Some days were simply too difficult, even as much as she loved him.

"Talk to me."

She dropped her chin, shaking her head as she hugged her legs tightly.

He dropped a kiss on her hair and emitted a deep sigh before sliding from the bed.

Tiffany kept her head bent and closed her eyes as the pain blossomed in her heart. Disappointing Aiden was the absolute worst feeling in the entire world. He'd tire of her soon if he hadn't already.

The click of the bathroom door closing was her cue. The tears broke free creating salty tracks down her cheeks. She pressed her face to her knees, unsuccessful in her attempt to control the shake of her shoulders as she sobbed.

"Tiff?" Aiden whispered.

How had he reappeared so soon and so stealthily?

"Why are you crying?" He tipped her chin up and forced her to look at him. A wrinkle appeared in his brow as he studied her with those deep brown eyes. "What's wrong? Tell me, and maybe we can fix it."

She gave the tiniest shake of her head and looked away, unable to stand his scrutiny. It felt like he saw inside her and knew how unlovable she truly was.

Aiden sighed. "If you won't talk to me ... I mean how will we survive this?" He exhaled a long slow breath. "Do you want to move back to Chicago, Tiff? Was this all a big mistake? I love you, but you're so unhappy, and it's killing me. If you don't want to be married ... to me ... you have to be honest and tell me."

"What?" She popped her head up. "No, no, Aiden. That's not it. I love you, and I want to be your wife, forever. It's hard because nobody is on our side."

"They'll come around. Don't worry."

"I hope they do." Tiffany gave him a watery smile. "Why aren't our friends happy and excited for us?"

"Give them time and they will be. In the meantime, let's have breakfast and enjoy the last of our holiday. Okay?"

She nodded and accepted his kiss. Time to stop worrying and enjoy being with the man she loved. It had taken far too long for him to come back to her.

"Morning." Tiffany swept into the kitchen with a big smile spread across her face. She stretched to press her lips to his, sighing against them. The love and tenderness this man displayed toward her every single day caused a warm tingle to rush through her body.

Aiden curled his arm around her, gazing into her eyes. "You're cheerful this morning."

She shrugged and grinned at him. "What should we do today? We have a couple more days before classes start."

Aiden's brows rose. "Really?"

He had a right to be surprised. Until yesterday, she'd allowed sadness to envelop her. For some crazy reason, she'd expected her family, especially her mother, to come around once her marriage to Aiden was fait accompli. That hadn't happened, but she still had what she wanted; Aiden. He'd taken the ultimate step to keep them together. That had to count for something.

The pain he'd exhibited over her continuous tears shook her from her despair. She never wanted him to think she regretted becoming his wife, or that she didn't love him enough to stay.

Tiffany threw a look at Will.

Their roommate sat at the table, scooping cereal into his mouth. "Don't mind me. I won't interfere with the rest of the honeymoon." He smirked.

"Sorry, Will. I've barged in."

Will rose from the table. "You're welcome here. If anyone is the interloper, it's me. I'm a little shocked over the married part." He shrugged and then leaned in to hug her and kiss her cheek. "I'm happy for both of you."

"You are?"

Will patted her back. "You've made Aiden a happy man. Who am I to bust that up?"

The ache in her heart receded, even if just a little. Her smile faded at the sound of a heavy knock on the door.

"Are we expecting someone?" Aiden asked.

Will shrugged as he shoveled in a mouthful of cereal.

Tiffany rubbed Aiden's arm as he passed by on the way to answer the door. She followed him, standing several feet back.

He swung it open. "Tom." Aiden crossed his arms. "Why are you here?"

"Can I come in?"

"It's not a great time."

"I drove all the way from New Haven. Please?"

Aiden sighed and stepped aside, beckoning Tom inside.

"Hi, Tiff." Tom pulled her in for a hug. "I heard the big news. Best wishes to you."

Tiffany peered up at Tom. "Thanks?"

Will stood and stretched before moving to place his bowl in the dishwasher. "I'll hit the shower."

Tom waited until Will had disappeared down the hall. "You've been dodging my calls." He squinted at Aiden.

"Maybe I have nothing to say." Aiden shrugged. "I'd hoped out of everyone that you'd understand, but nope, wrong again."

Tom sighed and bowed his head for a moment before straightening. "You're right. I'm sorry for reacting the way I did. If you're happy, I'm happy. I'd like to take you two out to celebrate. Forgive me?" He offered his hand.

Aiden frowned but then grasped his friend's hand. "Yeah. That would be great."

"Get ready." Tom waved them toward the upstairs as he headed toward the living room. "Don't take too long."

Within an hour, the three of them entered the restaurant. Tom gave his name and murmured something to the hostess, who smiled and pointed to a door at the side.

"Where are we going?" Tiffany whispered to Aiden as they followed their friend.

"Don't know?"

The moment they stepped through the door, she knew they'd been set up. Tears filled her eyes as she surveyed their group of friends. "You're all here." She glanced at Aiden and clutched his hand. "Did you know?"

He shook his head.

Moments later, she was surrounded by her friends and exchanging warm hugs as her eyes became misty.

Jenna handed her a drink. "Surprised?"

"Yes." She swept her fingertips underneath her eyes, brushing away the tears. "You're all here."

"Of course." Alex slid an arm around her waist. "We love you both, and wish you many years of joy."

"I love you guys. Thank you." She wrapped an arm around each of her friends, joy in her heart as she realized; this was all the family she needed.

Chapter 9

Aiden

Over the next six weeks, things settled into a normal routine. Or as much of one as he could manage now they'd both returned to school. On top of his classes, he'd been planning his summer activities, which, with any luck, would include a six-week summer surgical fellowship.

"I was hoping we'd go somewhere fun." A cute pout appeared on Tiffany's face as she surveyed the application package he'd brought home. "You want to hang around a hospital all summer?"

"It'll give me an advantage when I apply for residency." Aiden gave her a hopeful grin.

She shook her head as her eyes rolled toward the ceiling, but her lips twitched. With a saucy smile, she turned and scurried down the hall.

Instead of rushing after her, he stepped behind the door, waiting until the creak of the floor signaled she was on her way back. One thing he knew; Tiffany often lacked patience.

She peeked into the room, creeping in far enough for him to scoop her up by the waist and yank her against him. "Ha. Got you."

"Aiden." She struggled and wiggled free, laughing as she dashed from the room and bounded down the stairs toward the kitchen, her long blonde hair streaming behind her. "Now you don't." The taunt was thrown over her shoulder.

"You can't escape." He lunged after her, catching up in the dining room. Despite her attempt to circle the table and escape, he caught her and captured her soft warm lips in a long hot kiss.

Tiffany slid her flattened palms up his chest, looping an arm around his neck as she pressed her body against him. One hand crept into and ruffled his hair.

"Don't you two lovebirds ever give it a rest?"

Aiden threw a sideways glance at Will before planting another kiss on her, one arm curled around her slim waist.

"Guess that's a no." Will leaned on the counter. "Glad you're both here. Ben suggested I move into his place. He has an empty bedroom, and it's time I gave you two some privacy."

"You don't have to do that," Tiffany said. "You know you're welcome here."

Will shook his head. "It's time for the third wheel to go away. Besides, you two keep me awake half the damn night." He grinned. "So, end of the month?"

"No rush." Aiden waved his hand.

"Cool. I'm off to the library to study." He snagged a piece of cold pizza from the fridge and wandered toward his room.

"Where were we?" Aiden spanned her waist with his hands.

"We need to get ready for our date." Her eyes sparkled.

"Oh, that's tonight?" He lifted a brow, fighting to keep his lips from twitching.

She tossed her hair over her shoulder and strutted down the hall toward their bedroom.

Aiden followed, stepping inside as she peeled off her clothes and unhooked the slinky red dress from the hanger.

She slid the silky fabric over her hips. "Zip me up?"

Aiden swept her blonde waves aside before grazing his fingertips over the tattoo on her back. He traced the intricate design.

"You're supposed to be doing it up, not taking it off." Tiffany shivered. "We have reservations."

"I can't help it." After brushing his lips over the nape of her neck, gratified by the goosebumps on her flesh and the quiver that ran down her spine, he fastened her dress. "Your tattoo is drop-dead sexy. I'm glad you didn't chicken out."

She turned and gazed at him. "Yours is too."

Aiden caressed her cheek with the back of his hand. "You look beautiful, Tiff." He gazed at her, feeling like the luckiest man in the world. "Happy Valentine's, sweetheart."

Tiffany's head was bowed over her art table, her hair tied back in a messy bun, her long graceful neck exposed. The woman spent hours hunched over her work, painstaking in creating each and every intricate detail.

"Hey," he murmured, pressing a kiss to her exposed flesh.

A noticeable shiver ran down her spine and goosebumps rose on her arms. "Stop that, or I'll never get this finished." She giggled and gave him a playful shove.

"Sorry." He leaned over her, inspecting the design in front of her. "Amazing. You have an incredible eye, and it only gets better and better."

The woman had a true talent. She'd had a few art classes in her childhood years, but those were more about finger painting and crafts. Her formal training had been a few meager sessions in the art room at boarding school, the faculty of which was more interested in turning out future doctors and lawyers than encouraging creative pursuits. He noted the progression in her work, watching it go from good, to excellent, to incredible in the short time since she'd begun her tutelage under professionals.

"Thank you." She straightened and stretched her arms upward, swaying in her seat. "I plan to go out later and work on my composition." Her eyes lifted to meet his. "Thank you, Aiden. That's the best Valentine's present ever."

He squeezed her shoulder, grateful she appreciated the gift, which had been inspired by her struggles with her sub-par camera equipment. Though Tiffany loved jewelry, her eyes had lit up at the sight of the selection of high-end lenses and tripod that accompanied the top-of-the-line camera body.

"You should come."

"Sure. I could stand to get out of here for an hour or two." He rubbed at his gritty eyes. The hours of studying both the thick medical texts and peering at his computer screen created a blurring sensation. "Let me hop into the shower."

Within an hour, they were bundling up and heading into the snowy landscape. Aiden took the heavy camera bag from her and slung it over his shoulder before grabbing her gloved hand.

Her grateful smile and peck to his cheek made him smile in return. They trudged through the fresh snowfall, stopping now and again for Tiffany to capture a scene.

Everything felt perfect, a little window into what their life would be together. A future that stretched in front of them, endless and happy.

Tiffany tugged his arm, bringing him to a halt. "Don't change a thing." She stepped backward, one careful step at a time as she pointed the camera at him and adjusted her lenses. "Wait." The shutter clicked several times before she nodded. "Perfect."

After several more stops, some where she took more pictures of him, but many more of other subjects and scenes, she tucked her camera into her bag and rubbed her hands together. "It's cold. I'm ready to go home before my camera shutter freezes." She giggled.

"Or we could stop for hot chocolate." He encased her small hand in his large one. "Whipped cream?"

At her nod, they proceeded to one of the nearby cafés. Tiffany located a table while he ordered and delivered the steaming cups to their seats.

"I ordered some fries." He shrugged out of his coat and draped it over the back of his chair, tucking his gloves into one pocket.

"Eating again?" A grin appeared. "I think I got some fantastic shots today." She brought her cup up and took a ginger sip. "Mmm, delicious."

Aiden held back the smirk as he dragged a thumb across the corner of her mouth, catching a dab of cream. He licked it from his thumb. "That is pretty good."

"Ha ha, funny guy." She took another tiny sip from her cup. "We should catch a movie later. It's so rare that you have time off."

"Let's see what's playing."

They spent several minutes perusing the selections, finally coming to an agreement.

"Fries, Mommy. Fries." The shrill voice cut through the air.

They both turned their head at the same time, taking in the pair only a few feet away.

"Shush." The mother pressed a finger to her lips. "Quit shouting, honey. Are you hungry?" she asked as she removed the child's knit hat, releasing a cascade of lovely blonde ringlets.

Aiden estimated the little girl to be about four years old. His breath caught as she turned vivid blue eyes their way, and a picture flashed in his mind.

Tiffany clenched her hands around her cup, bowing her head as her teeth clamped onto her bottom lip.

"Tiff," he said softly.

She shook her head, angling her body away from the other table and keeping her gaze focused downward.

"We have to talk—"

"No." Her chin lifted the tiniest bit as she shot him a look. "Don't go there. How many times must I say it?" She shoved the dregs of her hot chocolate away and stood, grabbing her camera bag before she rushed for the door, pushing past the server heading their way with the order of fries. The small bell tinkled as she exited onto the street, striding away before Aiden had a chance to collect his coat and retrieve the beret his wife had abandoned on the edge of their table.

"Sir?" The teenage boy motioned to the basket in his hands.

Aiden shook his head even as his eyes focused on the mother and daughter at the nearby table. "Give them to the little girl." He dodged around the kid and headed onto the street. "Damn," he muttered.

She was already gone.

He zipped his coat and yanked out his gloves as he hurried in the direction she'd headed. If he was lucky, she'd be waiting at home. But when he arrived, the apartment was dark and silent. His calls went unanswered, so he left a brief message, hoping she'd either call him back or return to their home.

Nothing to do but wait. She could be anywhere. He slumped onto the couch, idly flicking through channels while his thoughts headed in another direction.

Tiffany's reaction to the little girl at the airport several months back hadn't escaped him. It seemed any little blonde child that fit the age group set her off. But no matter how many times he tried, she refused to discuss their past. It remained the dark spot in their relationship. The subject that could never be approached.

It made him wonder what their future held. He'd always pictured himself with a family, but perhaps that wasn't to be. All he could do was give her time to heal and hope for the best.

He tried calling her several more times and sent texts with no response. Eventually, he picked up one of his books and tried to study, but his mind kept wandering. Sitting here made him feel useless. He closed his eyes, draping the text across his chest.

A slight sound made him open his eyes. The apartment was dark except for the reading light over the couch, but he heard the click of a closing door.

He sat and rubbed a hand through his hair, squinting at the coat rack and spotting her wool winter coat before he rose and tiptoed up the stairs.

Sure enough, their bedroom door was closed, which meant she must be home. He rested his hand on the knob for a moment before opening it. "Tiff?" he whispered. When she didn't answer, he moved slowly toward the bed, stripping off his clothing and dropping it all onto the chair. He slid under the covers, hesitating before he spooned against her back and closed his eyes, one arm draped over her.

She said nothing, but linked her cold fingers through his, pressing their joined hands to her chest.

"Where did you go? You never called me back."

"Yeah, you seemed distraught, snoring away on the couch." A touch of bitterness colored her tone.

"It's three in the morning." He heaved a sigh and rolled away from her. "Never mind. Go to sleep."

"Now you're pissed at me?"

"You seem to be the pissed-off party even though you're the one who disappeared for hours. No explanation. No phone call. Not even a damn text message."

"I went to the art gallery downtown. After they closed, I went to see Bailey."

"You still could have called," he said. "Are we never going to talk about it?"

"What is there to say? There's no point. It just … hurts. Leave it be."

"Maybe talking about it would—"

"No."

"Did you talk about it with Bailey? Or with anyone?"

"No. This is your final warning. I don't wish to discuss it. Ever. So stop it."

"Where exactly does that leave us?"

"In the same spot we've always been and will always be. Let's just… get on with our lives." She wiggled closer and rested her head on his chest, her soft fingers trickling across his bare skin. "You take care of me. I take care of you. It's all we have left. It has to be enough."

Aiden pressed a kiss to the top of her head and curled an arm around her. It seemed he had no choice. If he pushed, he risked making it worse. If that was even possible.

Chapter 10
Tiffany

Regaining her equilibrium after that day in the café and her subsequent, albeit short, disappearance was a struggle. But her request to drop the discussion seemed to have gained the desired results. Her husband being an understanding and compassionate man certainly made it easier. He'd forgiven her or at least let her behavior slide.

As the snow melted and the early spring flowers broke through the earth, their married life blossomed. The pain of her family's rejection faded a little as she focused on her husband and her second love in life—her artwork.

"I'm off." He pressed a kiss to her lips, the light scent of aftershave combined with his minty breath, lingering as he straightened.

She peered at the clock through bleary eyes. "It's so early," she mumbled, already burying her head into her pillow. "And it's Saturday."

"No rest for us medical students. We have a lab to finish on top of that major exam on Monday. I'll be late tonight." After caressing her cheek with his fingertips, he slung his pack over his shoulder. "Bye, sweetheart." Seconds later, the soft click of the front door signaled he'd gone.

She sighed and lifted her arm in a long luxurious stretch. Further sleep would elude her, so she showered, clipped back her damp waves, and headed for the living room. The early morning sun cast a beam across the floor, flooding the open space with light.

She loved this cozy yet spacious apartment she shared with her husband. *Husband*. A soft smile touched her lips as she remembered their passionate lovemaking the night before, and the way their bodies entwined in the middle of the king-sized bed as they fell into an exhausted sleep. Now that Will had moved out, their sex life had heated up. Her inhibitions dropped away once there was no chance of interruption.

The half-finished sketch drew her eye. From experience, she understood *late* meant Aiden might reappear anytime between the hours of ten and midnight, so she'd make the most of her day and finish one of her own projects. But first, she needed to work out the kinks.

As she unrolled her yoga mat and began her morning stretches, her mind wandered to the ambitious young men and women comprising Aiden's lab and study groups, a smile twitching at her lips. "Bunch of keeners," she muttered.

The drive to succeed and battle their way to the top of their class seemed to be a common trait from what she'd observed whenever they'd studied here. And Aiden, being the youngest in his class by a full two years, worked even harder, certain he had something to prove.

Why he worried, she'd never understand. At eighteen, he'd been accepted into a prestigious Ivy League medical school after completing his undergraduate degree at Oxford. That put him far ahead of his peers, in her opinion.

With her morning routine completed, she poured her usual large cup of coffee. She perched at the art table positioned in front of the bank of large windows in the airy high-ceilinged main room. A critical eye cast on the work in front of her told her something wasn't jiving.

After spending an hour fussing with the design, she changed her clothes and packed her portfolio. Being alone wasn't something she could handle today, and the walk to the studio would be a welcome break.

"Hi, love." Bailey, her closest friend in Philly, planted a kiss on her cheek as she entered the art room. "What are you doing here?"

She lifted a shoulder and began the task organizing her workspace at the large table next to his.

"Is that fine husband of yours neglecting you again?" He winked.

"Always. But one day, he'll be an amazing doctor." She peered over his shoulder at the array of photos he had laid out. "Beautiful."

The young man had an amazing eye for detail, his love of being behind the lenses of a camera showing in every single photograph he took. No doubt this talented guy would excel in his career.

"Perhaps you'll model for me sometime." He looked at her. "Your husband won't mind, will he?"

"I doubt he'd take issue." The grin twitched at her lips. "Especially as you seem more attracted to him than to me."

"Well," her friend said with a snicker, "he is more my type. Too bad he's into girls."

Tiffany forced a stern look onto her face and wagged a finger. "Just one girl, thank you very much."

"You look happy today, so I guess he's been showing you just how completely devoted and madly in love he is, lucky girl." Bailey squeezed her hand. "You caught a good one, love." He rearranged a few of his images before glancing her way. "Have you heard from your family?"

"No, but that's not surprising. I'm sure my father is still stewing over the fact I disobeyed him. When he's upset and issues a decree, my mother goes along with it."

"Blackballed by your own family. I can relate to that, honey."

On the first day of class, she'd been drawn to Bailey. Over the weeks, they'd bonded and formed a close friendship. Unlike most of her classmates, who's chief complaints seem to be about the wicked stepmother or awful stepfather or wayward siblings, he understood how difficult life could be without any parents or siblings at all.

She offered him a faint smile as she adjusted her headphones and set to work. As usual, she became absorbed, barely glancing up as others entered the room and set up their own workstations. Art tended to be a solitary pursuit but sitting in a room of other like-minded individuals made her feel less lonely and isolated.

A soft tap on her shoulder had her looking up. With a smile, she tugged one of the earbuds free, accepting the take-away cup. "Thank you, Derrick, but you didn't have to do this."

"You're welcome." He leaned a hip against her table and tilted his head. "That's good"—he tapped an index finger on the corner of her page—"where did you find the inspiration? Can't be from Philly."

"Martha's Vineyard." If she closed her eyes, she could picture the long expanse of golden sand in front of Aiden's grandparents' beach house. Just around the bend, only a short stroll from the fire pit, was a lovely private spot where she'd shared many sunrises and sunsets with her friends. The winter storms might have washed it all away by now, but perhaps one day she'd revisit the site that held so many precious memories. "What are you working on?" She sipped the chai latte, savoring the light taste of cinnamon.

"Nothing quite as spectacular as that." His gaze traveled from the artwork to her left hand, and he motioned to the magnificent ring. "You never talk about him much. Doesn't your sugar daddy mind that you're always here instead of with him?"

A snort emitted from her left. "Sugar daddy?" Bailey threw a look their way. "Hardly."

"It's a big-ass diamond." Derrick captured her fingers, turning them as he inspected the intricate design on the ring. "Doesn't look like paste."

"No, it's real. And my husband, Aiden, is only a few months older than me." Tiffany giggled. "He's a medical student."

"Ahh. Well, that explains his lack of concern, I guess." A teasing grin appeared. "If you were my wife, I'd never let you out of my sight. Some guy might steal you away while he isn't looking." He winked again before strolling away and taking a seat at his own table.

Bailey arched a brow, his eyes cutting toward Derrick. A subtle shake of his head and barely perceptible eye roll said it all but he still mouthed the words, "Quit flirting."

Tiffany snickered as she bent her head and refocused on adding details.

Derrick's alluring blue eyes, sandy-blond hair, and chiseled features were certainly attractive. And the way his jeans hugged his tight ass and how his broad shoulders and firm chest filled out his snug t-shirt didn't hurt the view, but the flirtation meant nothing. She loved Aiden. No other man could replace what she shared with her husband. Besides, her guy was a certified hottie in his own right.

The constant love and support shown by her own man made the attentions of others pale in comparison.

She shot a quick look across the room, ducking her head as she caught Annalise's scathing look. Their classmate always gave Tiffany the stink-eye when she spoke to Derrick, and clearly, she'd heard the flirtatious comments. "He's all yours, honey," she muttered, focusing on her sketch. As flattering as the attention was, Aiden was her man.

───

By the first week of June, Tiffany was bored. It had been no surprise to her when Aiden had accepted a surgical fellowship for the summer. All of her classmates had disappeared to visit family or take jobs to offset the expenses for next year's tuition.

With the long hours Aiden put in at the hospital, she was often left to entertain herself. She cursed herself for not seeking an internship. Technically, she didn't have to work. For some unknown reason Gramma Grace had continued to cover the rent on their apartment and the wages of the housekeeper, Erika, who cleaned and stocked the fridge on a weekly basis.

This left her with both mixed feelings and little to do around their home. Her husband shared the financial security he enjoyed, never demanding money for anything and even paying her tuition without a single complaint. His generosity made her feel loved and cherished. But it also carried a modicum of guilt. She longed to find other ways to contribute and to become a woman who deserved this wonderful man who, despite their economic differences, treated her like his equal in everything.

Time to do something about it. She chose a light business-casual dress and paired it with dressy sandals, leaving her hair to fall in soft waves around her shoulders. After tucking her sadly lacking resume in a folder, she headed into the bright summer morning.

By noon, her feet ached and she felt completely discouraged. Every single place she received either a smile with a head shake or a frown as she presented her resume. In Chicago, her father had never encouraged her to work so she had nothing to boast about aside from one year of education and her artwork.

Time to go home and call my day a failure. She swung her folder, occasionally fanning herself with it as she ambled along the sidewalk. A picture displayed in the window of one of her favorite galleries caught her eye, and she halted, stepping closer to admire it. "Beautiful." She sighed and tugged open the door. What she needed was a distraction and some inspiration after a mildly depressing day.

"Tiffany. What are you doing here?" The familiar man looked up from where he was cleaning a display.

"Derrick. You work here?"

"Had to do something over the summer." He grinned. "I'm not living the lifestyle of the rich and famous." His eyes traveled over her. "You look good. What were you up to?"

"Job hunting?" She shrugged. "Aiden earned a fellowship, so he's buried in scut work at the hospital. I've left it too late and ... my resume sucks," she whispered.

"Derrick. Have you seen Ellen? Or heard from her?" The short, slight man in a bespoke suit hurried across the floor.

"Nope, sorry."

"She's late. Again." He threw his hands in the air. "I need her to help set up for the show tomorrow. When she gets here, tell her she's fired." The well-dressed guy shook his head.

"Gabe ... this is Tiffany. She's in my class." He winked.

Gabe stepped toward her, holding out his hand. "My apologies. I'm a little stressed as you can tell." The man tilted his head. "You go to school with Derrick? How much do you know about art?"

"Some. I do love that painting in the front window. Incredible use of shape and color. This is a beautiful gallery."

"You wouldn't happen to be looking for a job, would you? I could really use some help. As you've gathered, my other employee is none too reliable."

"Really?" Tiffany smiled, her heart lightening.

"It doesn't pay much, and it requires a lot of work in the evenings but ..."

"She doesn't mind, do you, Tiff?" Derrick grinned. "Her husband is a medical student, so he's never home."

Tiffany fought the urge to roll her eyes at him and smiled at Gabe instead. "I would love to get some experience in a gallery."

"Can you start right away? Like … now?" The man arched a brow.

"I can. Show me where to put my things, and tell me what you need me to do."

Working at the gallery gave Tiffany a purpose. And she enjoyed having full access to the beautiful display of paintings and artwork on an almost daily basis, even if the work wasn't as glamorous as she'd assumed. She didn't even mind the long hours as Aiden was often at the hospital until late at night. And the camaraderie amongst their small team made her feel like she had gained a family at last. Mostly, she was happy and she loved her husband. But, just as things were going well, a dark spot appeared.

"Hi, honey," Bailey said as he appeared in the gallery in late August.

"What are you doing here?" Tiffany threw her arms around him. "I thought you were gone until classes started?"

"I came back to pack my things," he said. "I have some news. The Art Institute in Chicago accepted me. I start in September."

Tiffany frowned. "But you can't leave. What will I do without you?"

"I'll miss you too, love." He held out his arms. "This is an amazing opportunity for me."

She nodded with a sad smile. "I understand, Bailey. I am really going to miss you."

"We'll keep in touch, I promise. I wanted to tell you in person, but I have to go as my ride to Chicago is waiting." With a final warm hug and a wave, he headed out the door.

As happy as she was for her friend, his departure made her sad. She'd given up her own spot at the Art Institute and now, her closest friend in Philly would be gone.

"Don't worry. You still have me." Derrick leaned against the front counter, awarding her a cheeky smile.

"Mmmhmm." Tiffany wound a finger into her hair and tugged firmly.

"Well, thanks." He rolled his eyes before shoving a cloth and spray bottle of glass cleaner at her. "The displays need cleaning."

She threw him a dark look. It seemed that was all she did lately. Clean the gallery. "Fine. Go do"—she fluttered her fingers—"whatever it is you do."

"I work hard, thank you very much." He spun and strutted toward the crate that needed unpacking, sending a saucy grin her way.

Tiffany shook her head and headed in the opposite direction, resigned to yet another round of dusting.

Chapter 11

Aiden

Summer turned into fall, with even busier schedules than before. They'd managed a short holiday to Maine for a romantic interlude in the mountains during the last week of summer, but after that, they'd had far less time together.

Tiffany seemed content with both her classes at the art school and with her continuing work at the small gallery downtown. When he'd heard about her new job, he'd encouraged her to take full advantage of the opportunity. The upside was he felt less guilty about his crazy hours. The downside was when he made it home at a reasonable hour, she would still be at work.

Another benefit was her schedule kept her sidetracked so she wasn't worrying about her nineteenth birthday. She'd heard nothing from her family since the day they were married, and Bailey's move to Chicago had proven to be a tough blow.

"Happy birthday, sweetie." He planted a kiss on her lips as he served her the fluffy omelet and fresh-squeezed orange juice while she lounged in their bed.

"Yum." She patted the mattress beside her. "Join me?"

"I wish I could, but class starts in"—he glanced at his watch—"twenty minutes. I'll see you tonight, right?"

"I can't wait." Her bright smile lightened his heart.

After he'd finished his classes for the day, he picked up the birthday cake he'd ordered, along with a dozen red roses and dressed in dark-washed jeans and a button-down shirt. Then he gathered the bouquet and the gift before heading down to meet her at the gallery.

"Aiden." Tiffany hurried over as he stepped inside. She pressed a kiss to his lips before glancing at her watch. "Is it that time already?" Her gaze wandered to the pile of crates at the far end of the space.

"You're not done?"

"I'm so sorry." She shook her head. "The shipment arrived late, and now we're scrambling to finish the displays. I lost track of the time, or I would have called."

"I understand." The same scenario happened to him with his studies, making it impossible to be upset with her.

"Is that for me?" She motioned to the box.

"Happy birthday." Aiden handed her the flowers. "And this," he said as he held up the gift bag, "but you can open it later." The feeling of being inspected rose and he cast a glance toward where Gabe and Derrick were hanging a large piece of artwork.

Derrick's gaze met his for only a second before the man looked away, avoiding Aiden's narrowed eyes. The few brief interactions he'd had with the other man hadn't made him a fan. Aiden hated how the guy talked to and looked at his wife.

"These are gorgeous," Tiffany said as she peeked inside the box, oblivious to the tension between him and the other man. "I'm so sorry about dinner." A hand crept up and she caught a lock of her hair, twisting it around her finger and tugging.

"It's fine. You have to work. I get it." He caught her around the waist, giving her a long deep kiss.

"Mmm, a little sugar," she murmured against his lips. "Hold that thought until I get home."

"You bet I will," he whispered against her ear. "Happy birthday."

After leaving the gallery, he went home to put the roses in water and leave the gift for her on the counter. Will had mentioned some of the guys were heading to the local pub to play pool and drink beer, so he decided he'd join them. There was no point in hanging around the apartment alone.

"Surprised to see you here." Ben raised his brows as Aiden slid into the booth. "I thought you had a hot date."

"She bailed. Tomorrow is opening night for some artist, and they're still setting up."

"Isn't it her birthday?" Will waved at the waitress.

"Yeah, but I had a shift on my birthday too, so …" He shrugged. "So, I missed dinner. I'll eat and then we should play pool."

Throughout the evening, Aiden took small breaks between games to call Tiffany, but by midnight, she was still at work. When he arrived home at two, their bed was empty. It wasn't until three a.m. that she arrived home and crawled in beside him.

"Hey," he muttered sleepily. "You get it all done?"

"Finally." She brushed his lips with hers. "I'm exhausted." Tiffany rolled over and buried her head in her pillow, asleep within moments.

He closed his own eyes, willing himself to get some rest so he could be up at his usual time of five. Soon something would have to give. He wasn't sure how long they could manage this balancing act when they barely spent any time together.

Over the next months, things didn't get any easier. Winter arrived, along with their first anniversary as a married couple. This year, instead of a luxurious and relaxing vacation on the beach, Aiden was faced with exams and a wife who was busy with her own schooling and part-time job.

"Happy anniversary," he said as he rose for another day of classes. "I'm sorry we can't go out tonight to celebrate. The exam tomorrow is over fifty percent of our grade."

"I understand." She accepted his kiss, wrapping her arms around his neck. "I need some sugar. I miss you." Pearly white teeth clamped onto her lower lip as she batted her crystal blue eyes.

"Maybe I could skip my workout."

A smile twitched her lips. "Oh, don't worry about that." She wiggled her brows. "You'll get in your exercise."

When he arrived a class a full two hours late, he couldn't hide his contented grin as he slipped into his customary seat.

Will narrowed his eyes and then a smirk appeared, but Aiden was saved from his comments as the professor began their lecture. But at the end of the class, Will tapped his watch. "A little late today, weren't you? What kept you?"

Aiden simply lifted his brows and smiled.

"Never mind then." Will smothered a grin. "I remember what it was like living with you two."

He shrugged but noted that Matthias had a sad expression marring his features. "What's up?" he asked as Will and the rest of their study group funneled toward the door.

"Nothing." His friend shoved his books into his bag.

"I don't believe that." Aiden put a hand on the man's arm to hold him back. "Are you still having issues with Tess?"

"She dumped me."

"I'm sorry." Aiden blew out a puff of air. His friend had been struggling for the past two months. Living far from home and missing his girl was something he could relate to on a personal level. "Only a few days and you'll be home for the holidays. Maybe you can talk to her and—"

"Never. The relationship received the kiss of death." Matthias curled his lip. "She said it isn't me, it's her."

"Man." Aiden cringed at the cliché break-up line. "That's rough. Anything I can do?"

"Let it go. I decided not to go home this year. Small town and all that. We have the same friends. So … yeah."

"Well, Tiff and I are hosting at our place, so you could come over. Ben and Will might stay as well, and we'll go skiing between Christmas and New Year's."

Matthias shrugged.

"I won't take no for an answer. If you don't show up, then we'll drag you."

"Do I have to?" he said. "I'd rather eat pizza and play video games."

"You can do that at our house. Or at least eat amazing snacks with the video games."

The man sighed. "Fine. Let me know what time and I'll be there."

"Any time after noon. You know where we live." Aiden motioned to the door. "The guys are waiting for us to join the study session."

Matthias gave him a faint smile. "Yeah, let's get this over with."

Aiden didn't arrive home until one in the morning, and all he wanted to do was sleep. His exam started at nine and would last for at least four hours.

"You're finally home." Tiffany rolled toward him. "I tried waiting for you, but I got so sleepy."

"Sorry, but we had a good study session. I should do well on tomorrow's exam."

Tiffany cuddled against his chest. "My brilliant husband will pass at the top of the class. I just know it."

"Thanks for your confidence in me." Aiden brushed his lips against hers. "What did you do all evening?"

"I worked at the gallery. Then Derrick invited me for coffee."

The thought that his wife spent their anniversary with another man caused his gut to twist. Especially since it was Derrick. That man already enjoyed more time with his wife than he did. A deep sigh escaped him. "I thought you were working on your art, not going out with another guy."

"He's a colleague and a classmate. Why are you so upset? I was patient about the fact that you had to study on our anniversary. What? I'm supposed to sit around waiting for you?" She scoffed and presented her back to him. "Don't be such a jerk," she muttered.

"I don't like you spending so much time with him. You see him in class every day, you work with him, and now he's taking you on dates?"

"We had coffee." She sat and crossed her arms. "If you don't want me going out with other people, then try being home once in a while." With a glare in his direction, she swung her feet to the floor and stomped toward the door. "Such an asshole."

This woman was exhausting. Nobody became a doctor without paying the toll. But he wouldn't let this go. He hauled himself out of bed and headed toward the stairs, following the faint sound of music carrying from the living room. She'd labeled it as her melancholy music mix, and he wondered if he'd been too harsh with her. He hesitated for a moment, taking in the solitary figure perched on the stool in front of her art table. The dim light from her lamp caught the gold highlights in her hair, making her look like an angel. An angelic figure who sniffled and dabbed at her eyes as her pencil scraped against the paper.

"Don't cry." He moved behind her, wrapping his arms around her waist and squeezing. "I'm sorry. I'm just tired."

"No, you're unreasonable. And acting jealous for no reason." She tipped her head, revealing her shimmering eyes. "Don't you trust me?"

"Of course, I trust you. Don't be silly." *It's him I don't trust.*

"Then why are you angry?" she whispered. "I've done nothing wrong. My heart aches when you're not here. Bailey is gone, you're busy, Jenna and Alex live in other states, and I haven't grown close to many of the girls in my class. Derrick is the only one who is nice to me."

Maybe these tears were about more than missing her friends. It might have to do with her mother and the lack of communication with her since the wedding. As difficult as Michelle Baxter could be, he knew she loved her daughter. "Why don't you call her?"

"Who?" A furrow appeared in her brow.

"Your mom. You haven't spoken to her in months."

She blinked hard and wagged her head back and forth. "Never. My family made their choice to cut me from their lives. I can never go home."

"You don't know that, Tiff—"

"I don't? My mother has never called or even sent me a damn birthday card since the day we told her we were married. That sends a pretty clear message. I'm the family embarrassment, and I'm not welcome. Do you even know how that feels?"

He closed his eyes and bowed his head, forcing down the sorrow in his own heart. The feeling of abandonment he understood all too well.

"Aiden." She rose, cupping his face between her palms. "I'm sorry for saying that."

"Never mind, Tiff. We knew from the start how this would go with our families. All we have is each other, and I'm sorry for that." He pulled her against him, pressing his face into her hair.

There was only one way to rectify this untenable situation. Tomorrow he would phone his mother-in-law to arrange a visit. This entire move had been tough on his new wife, and he would find a way to make it up to her.

"I'll try to contain my jealousy, even though it won't be easy." He brushed his lips against her cheek. "We'll take a break at Christmas, I promise. Come to bed." Aiden reached over her shoulder and turned off the desk lamp, grasping her warm fingers between his own and tugging her to her feet. He scooped her up in his arms and carried her upstairs, enjoying the soft warmth of her body against his. Once he reached their room, he laid her gently on the bed, hovering over her and dropping kisses on her.

"I love you, Aiden." She curled her arms around his neck. "We'll be okay, won't we?"

"Don't worry." Aiden nuzzled his face against her neck, enjoying the sweet smell of her perfume. This was his favorite scent in the entire world, one he gifted her. "You smell delicious."

He grazed his fingers over her silky skin, enjoying the soft sigh that left her lips. Losing himself in this woman was so damn easy. He knew he'd love her forever.

The next day, once he'd completed the long exam, he found a quiet corner to make his call. "Please don't hang up," he said the moment the feminine voice answered.

"Why are you calling?" she whispered. "Is Tiffany okay?"

"She's not injured or anything." He heaved a sigh. "She misses you. Is there any way you could visit her? Or can she come there? I'll pay for her flight."

"No, I can never come to Philadelphia," she said in a low voice. "You can't be calling me. What if David overheard?"

"What if he did?" He scrubbed a hand through his hair and sank onto a nearby bench. "She's your daughter, but she's afraid to call home because of how it all went down. Is your husband going to prevent you from ever speaking to her again?"

"No, not if she ...." Michelle's intake of breath was audible. "There are conditions to her coming home. You won't like them."

Aiden scoffed. "Oh, I see. So, what? She leaves me and she'll be welcomed into the Baxter family again? Is that it?"

The awkward silence confirmed his suspicions.

"You know that will never happen. I'm sorry to have bothered you. I won't call again."

"Aiden—"

Her words cut off as he disconnected. They were truly on their own. And even worse, he could never share this call with his wife. Suspecting the rejection of her family was one thing, but confirming it irrevocably was something else altogether. He couldn't stand the thought of breaking her heart.

Chapter 12

Tiffany

The savory smells wafted to her nostrils as she stretched and rose from her bed. Aiden had risen early and set to work after telling her to stay in bed and sleep in after a late night at the gallery.

Even though her husband had grown up privileged, he was an amazing chef. She managed in the kitchen, but Aiden was a master at preparing incredible gourmet meals.

After a quick shower, she headed downstairs, running her fingers across his back on her way to the coffee machine. "Morning, my love."

"Hey, sweetie." He smiled at her before turning back to his task. "Sleep well?"

"Mmmhmm. It was marvelous." Once she had a cup, she slid an arm around his waist, peering at the apple pie he was preparing. "Wow. You missed your calling. All those months on a sailboat taught you well."

"It did, but my grandmother's cook, Julissa, gets the majority of the credit."

"How so?" She stole a piece of the apple mixture, a twinge appearing in her chest as she remembered how she stole tidbits when her mother baked.

"When I was young, the kitchen fascinated me. That mansion was a lonely place for an only child, and you know how warm and cuddly my mother is. Whenever my parents dumped me there for a weekend, I would gravitate to Julissa. I don't know if you remember her or not, but she was this motherly woman who would bake me cookies and make me hot chocolate."

The pang in her heart grew. A picture of Aiden as a small boy wandering alone in that big mansion, neglected by his parents and ignored by his grandfather, grew in her mind. She blinked back the tears and forced a smile. "So you absorbed it by osmosis?"

He let out a chuckle. "No. She put me to work, giving me little things to do to help. As I got older, she taught me more, and I grew to love cooking. It's like this tiny happy spot in my childhood. The kitchen was a place I could be a kid and make a mistake without being berated."

"You've never told me this before. Why?" Tiffany leaned closer, enjoying the warmth of his arm as it curled around her waist.

"I don't know." He frowned. "It's almost a sacred memory, I guess. And I don't want people to judge me. I've had so much, Tiff, and complaining about my parents or how awful it was in that house …" Aiden lifted a shoulder.

"The silver spoon syndrome." Her mind traveled to the first night she'd sneaked from the dorms, and his overreaction to an innocent comment she'd made about him wanting something from her.

"Pretty much. People don't understand the hole it leaves in your life when you feel"—his frown deepened—"unwanted. To them, having a child was something they were obligated to do. A check mark on their list of life accomplishments. All people see is the insane amount of money at my disposal and assume it makes up for my crappy childhood."

She turned and peered into his eyes as she flattened her palm to his chest, directly over his heart. "I don't," she whispered. "All I see is a man with a beautiful generous heart, combined with an endless capacity to love me, as imperfect as I am." Those deep brown eyes drew her in, causing her pulse rate to increase.

He tangled a hand in her hair, bringing his head down to bestow the gentlest of kisses. "You're my perfect woman," he murmured against her mouth. "Forever, Tiff. What we have is forever." His warm minty breath wafted across her cheek before he captured her lips again.

Those words echoed in her mind as she wove her fingers into the silky strands of his hair. *My perfect forever man.* She sucked in a breath as he rested his forehead against hers, stroking her cheek with his thumb. "Aiden—"

The sound of the door buzzer shattered the moment.

"That'll be the guys." Aiden planted a kiss on her before he drew back. "Merry Christmas, sweetheart."

She patted his cheek before turning toward the door. "You keep working on the dinner preparations and I'll let them in."

Within two minutes, Will, Ben and Matthias were crowding through the door, and her hostess duties began.

To her surprise, the day was enjoyable. They had a small gift exchange, then an afternoon of snacks and games, followed by an elaborate prime rib dinner.

"Sit." She waved at Aiden as he rose to clear the table after the meal. "You've done so much. Let me take care of the clean up."

"I'll help." Matthias gathered a stack of plates, following her into the kitchen. He loaded the dishwasher as Tiffany stowed the leftovers in the fridge.

"Why didn't you go home for the holidays?" she asked.

Matthias shrugged. "I'm not in the mood to celebrate." He swept his fingers through his dark wavy hair. "Aiden didn't tell you?"

"No." She glanced at the man from the corner of her eye, noting the downturn of his mouth. "What happened?"

"The usual. My girlfriend dumped me. I don't want to hang around everyone who knew us as a couple. Dating someone who is so close with all of your friends and then breaking up really sucks."

"I can imagine. I'm sorry."

"Why didn't you go home?" he asked.

"Our families dumped us right after we got married."

"Harsh." He leaned against the counter. "Aiden never really talks about his family, though I gather his father is some big shot lawyer in New York. What does yours do?"

"He's running for mayor in Chicago for the second time." She brushed her hair back from her face.

"Why is your marriage an issue?"

Tiffany shrugged. "I have never figured it out. There's bad blood between my father and his for some unknown reason. I've asked, but my parents avoid the discussion. They simply demanded I break off the relationship for my own good. Whatever that means."

"My family loves Tess. I haven't even told them we broke up, but by now, they probably know." He sighed. "We promised we would get through the separation and that we would love each other forever."

She nodded, unsure of what to say. That echoed the reassurances she and Aiden gave each other on a regular basis.

"It's good you two are together, even if your family disapproves. I would give anything to be with Tess now, but I also can't bear seeing her face. It would hurt too much."

"Maybe that would make the difference, though. What if seeing you made her realize …" Tiffany bit her lip. "Sorry, that's none of my business. I'll shut up now."

"It's fine." He offered a sad smile. "I thought about it, you know. But"—he shrugged—"she told me to stay away. So I am. I feel like I've lost my friends too, you know?"

"Hey, you two, almost done?" Aiden wrapped his arms around her from behind. "Come join us."

"Almost finished." She leaned into him. This man was her everything. The trouble Matthias was having with his girlfriend, Tess, highlighted just how lucky she was to have Aiden.

By one in the morning, they were all yawning and their three friends said goodnight and headed home. Tiffany moved around the apartment, tidying up the few remaining plates and glasses scattered across the surfaces.

"I'll finish here. Turn off the lights and get ready for bed." Aiden brushed his lips over her cheek before steering her out of the kitchen.

She wandered toward the brightly lit Christmas tree, running a fingertip over each ornament. Aiden had gifted her another this year as a memento of their second holiday as a couple. She loved the idea that every year they were together would be marked in this small way.

"Hey." His arms curved around her and she leaned into his chest, tipping her head back to peer up at him. "Did you have a good day?"

She offered a soft smile and tiny nod as she placed her hands over his. Despite a lingering sadness that she still hadn't heard anything from her family, she counted her blessings. Her husband was wonderful and caring which were qualities her father lacked.

"You and Matthias seemed to have a good chat," he said.

"He's sad about Tess," she said. "I spoke out of turn and suggested he go home to visit her and maybe get her back. I hope I didn't make it worse."

"I told him the same thing, but his feelings seem too raw at the moment. It's understandable. Look how it is for Joel and Alex. It's awkward when we get together as a group now they've broken up."

Her mind traveled to the comment Matthias had made about the friend situation he faced at home. "Yeah, that's what Alex said. I miss them." She sighed and closed her eyes, thinking of how it used to be in the early days of dating Aiden when their group was inseparable over the holidays. It seemed strange now that their friends were in various relationships and scattered across the country. Maybe one day they would all live in the same city and regain the closeness that had faded in their absence.

Aiden rocked them on their feet, his cheek pressed to hers as a comfortable silence fell over them.

"I'm going to call my mom," she whispered. "Would it be okay if I invited her for a visit?"

"No." He tensed, his grip on her tightening as he cleared his throat. "It's not a good idea, sweetie. Besides, we planned to go skiing for a few days, so maybe you should wait until things settle down after the break."

She turned in his arms, a frown appearing as she studied his expression. "You've been all about me calling her for months, and now when I say I will, you're saying no? What's with you?"

His lips set into a flat line for only a second before a tense smile appeared. "Nothing. It's just that we won't have another chance to get away until after the next round of exams in April."

If she hadn't been watching closely, she would have missed the flicker of guilt in his eyes. "You're hiding something." She stepped back. "Don't lie to me, Aiden. I can spot it a mile away. You've never been good at keeping things from me."

"I'm not hiding anything." He caught her around the waist and dragged her toward him, dipping his head to catch her lips.

Her pulse rate quickened as she looped an arm around his neck, sinking into his embrace. There was something he didn't want her to know. She felt it with absolute certainty, but they'd had an amazing day, and starting a fight now would ruin it. When her temper flared, it created a rift between them for hours, and sometimes even days, so for now, she'd let him have his way. There would be time to broach the subject again soon. One way or another, she'd pry the truth from him. She always did in the end.

Chapter 13

Aiden

January and February rushed by with even longer hours of study and more time in the lab with his study group. He was glad he'd managed to coerce Tiffany into the short ski holiday in December as he'd had little time to spend with her since.

His wife spent more and more hours at the gallery and seemed immersed in her classes, though he suspected she spent too much time alone. With Bailey now in Chicago, he worried about her isolating herself.

This summer would be a busy one, and he'd have even less time for Tiffany. Aiden sighed and stretched out on the roof top lounger, tapping his pencil as he perused the chart. Now the weather had warmed up, he spent as much time as possible outdoors, even if he usually had a textbook in his hands with his laptop open nearby.

"What are you working on now?" Tiffany appeared and slumped into a chair beside him. Her pale legs peeked out from a pair of short shorts, and she twined a lock of hair around her finger, tugging at it.

Aiden glanced at her. "I have to sort out the labs and rotations I need to fit in this summer."

"What?" She frowned. "I kind of hoped …"

He caught the shiny glint in her eyes as she turned away. "Hey, what's wrong?" He sat upright and planted his feet on the patio.

She shrugged and yanked on her hair.

Aiden moved across to sit beside her, capturing her hand and freeing it from her hair. "When you do that I know something's up, Tiff." He ran his gaze down her body. "You've lost more weight."

Tiffany had never been big, but now he was concerned. Her former slim softness had become gaunt angles.

"I have the summer off, and I hoped we'd have some time together for a vacation. We haven't had much time together since the Christmas holidays." She pulled her arms in close to her body and shivered.

"You're cold." He rubbed her arm before peeling off his sweater and tugging it over her head. "I promise we'll go away for at least a week. I can work out my schedule to give us a vacation, and I'll do my best to get into the programs offered here in Philly. Some of the guys are trying to land closer to home for theirs."

"I guess it won't be Italy this summer." She tucked her hands into the overly long sleeves, bringing her legs up and wrapping her arms around them.

Aiden quelled his irritation. The woman was obsessed with this fantastic trip to Europe. "I'm sure you'll be spending time at the gallery, right? And you could take business classes over the summer to keep yourself busy."

"Business?" She wrinkled her nose.

"Successful gallery owners need to know how to run a business, Tiff. With your grades and my connection with the university, I'm sure you'd be admitted."

"I'll manage to keep busy. Don't worry." Tiffany stroked his cheek. "I love you."

Her abrupt change in demeanor worried him, but he didn't want to push. That could only bring her anger rushing to the surface. "I'll make sure I take at least a week off, I promise." He linked their fingers. "I'm sorry this is so difficult, but when I'm done—"

"You'll be a fabulous doctor." The smile that touched her lips seemed more sad than joyful at that pronouncement.

"And in the meantime, you'll become an amazing artist. One day, you'll own a huge gallery. Maybe in New York."

"Or Chicago. It would be nice to be close to our friends again."

"Sounds perfect."

Over the next two weeks, things leveled out and Tiffany seemed to find more to keep herself busy. Aiden was grateful as final exams were coming up, and he was buried by the amount of studying.

He shut the front door with a soft click, taking a moment to find a vase for the flowers he'd picked up earlier and set them in the center of the table with the bakery box beside them. When she found them in the morning, she would remember how much he loved her, even when he seemed irritated and out of sorts.

With a deep sigh, he cleared off the granite island and dumped her dinner leftovers in the trash before loading the scattered dishes into the dishwasher. *I love her even when she irritates me*, he reminded himself as he glanced at the bright bouquet. Lately, he'd been coming home to an apartment in disarray. Erika came in regularly to clean and stock their fridge and pantry, but in between times, Tiffany left dirty dishes and discarded food packaging strewn across every surface. It drove him crazy.

The front door opened as he was about finished wiping the counters. "Hey. I thought you were asleep."

"Nope." She giggled as she leaned against the wall, wobbling as she fought with her shoes. With her back pressed against the door, she kicked repeatedly until her high-heeled shoe flew and hit the wall with a thunk before tumbling to the floor.

"What the—" He shot a look her way before his gaze traveled to the mark left by the slender heel. "Careful with the walls. And maybe you could clean up after yourself once in a while."

"Oh, relax." Another giggle broke free as she kicked off her other shoe, grinning as it arced in the air and landed with a clunk on the wood floor. "You used to be more fun."

With a glower in her direction, he flipped off the kitchen light. "It's two in the morning. I'm exhausted, and I come home to crap all over the kitchen and you arriving home half wasted. Sorry I can't be out partying with you and your artist friends." A frisson of anger appeared as a picture formed in his mind of her out with Derrick. "Maybe try arriving home at a decent hour."

"That's rich, coming from the guy who just walked in the door."

"I'm busting my ass to finish my education and make something out of my life." He rolled his eyes. "I'm not out partying and drinking beer like all those artists you hang around with."

"My friends aren't good enough? We're all silly artists?" Fire erupted in her eyes as she stalked toward him.

"I didn't say that. Not even close. I already did the undergrad thing and—"

"Yada, yada, whatever." She shoved at his chest with her flattened palms. "I've heard this a million times." With a final push, she spun and stomped into the living room. "Maybe if you paid me some attention, I wouldn't be out finding it elsewhere."

Aiden followed, planting his feet and crossing his arms, the heat of anger rising, making his entire body quiver. "And just what sort of attention are you finding?" He clenched a fist but kept his voice flat and level. "I bet Derrick is all over that." *And all over you.*

"Oh, grow up. I gave up the Art Institute to move and be with you, but you're never here."

"Quit acting like a spoiled child. I'm paying for you to have a good education. If you don't like it, pack your bags and go home to Mommy and Daddy." Aiden shook his head. "I'm exhausted and have to be up at five."

Tiffany narrowed her eyes and grasped the colorful bouquet from the table, launching it at him with incredible force for such a slender woman.

Aiden dodged as the vase struck the wall behind him. The glass shattered and water dribbled to the floor. "What the fuck?" He picked a tiny shard of glass from his arm and squinted at her.

"Now that I have your attention"—Tiffany shoved her hair back from her pink face—"fuck you and your jealousy."

"What? Are you two?" He covered the few steps between them.

She raised her chin, her breasts heaving as her hand rose. The resounding slap across his face echoed through the open space. "Like you care." The tears cascaded down her cheeks and her bottom lip quivered. Tiffany struck out again, sobbing as he grabbed her wrists and pulled them down to her sides.

"Stop. Tiffany, just …" He dragged in a breath. "Please. Stop," he whispered.

She bowed her head, her shoulders sagging. "I don't want to go."

As the fight and anger drained out of her, he felt safe to release her wrists and slide his arms around her trembling body.

A sniffle broke free as she lifted her arms, her flattened palms moving upward to rest on his chest. "I love you," she whispered as she lifted her face and peered at him from under her wild mop of blonde waves. Her eyes shimmered, her face crumpling as the tears gathered in her eyes.

"Don't cry, sweetheart." He brushed away the first salty drop that trickled down her cheek with his thumb before cupping her face and kissing her.

"Aiden," she murmured against his lips as her soft hands grazed across his bare skin. Her willing form pressed against him, and she twined a hand into his hair, increasing the pressure of their mouths.

The desire grew within him. She never failed to draw him in with her softness and warmth. Even more so when they fought. *Strange and dysfunctional.* On some level, he understood how unhealthy this volatile side of their relationship could be, but he felt powerless to stop. This woman was wild and unpredictable. Untamable. And did he truly want to quell that fiery, passionate side of this temptress that he loved beyond reason?

Some days were a struggle, but he accepted her as she was—a deep complicated well of emotions that bubbled up without warning. In return, she'd always loved him despite his many faults and complicated family situation. He ran a hand over her hip, catching the bottom of her sweater and working it over her head.

Her fingers fumbled at the front of his shirt before she gave it an impatient tug, freeing several buttons. The warmth of her hands pressing on his chest made him shiver, but they lingered only a moment before dropping to the closure of his jeans. Tiffany tipped her head to the side, exposing the soft flesh of her throat as she tugged at the denim.

Aiden brushed her long hair away, tracing a pathway up the silky skin before capturing her lips. He curved his hands under her butt, lifting her and turning to settle her on the counter.

She emitted a soft, enticing moan as she wrapped her legs around him. "I've only ever been with you." Her breathless words wafted against his ear and her voice trembled. "I waited for you, Aiden. You're it for me. Everything. For always."

The words spun through his mind. He'd never imagined that for all those years of separation this woman had remained his. Only his. He sucked in a breath and grasped her face, sending out a silent vow to the universe to be more patient and gentler with this woman who'd endured so much, yet remained a strong and vital part of his life.

"And you're it for me. Forever, Tiff." He poured all of his love for her into this moment, twining his fingers through her hair as they shared kisses. *Forever. Always.*

Chapter 14

Tiffany

The entire marriage idea hadn't turned out anything like Tiffany had expected. *Naive on my part.* When she'd said yes to Aiden's proposal, she'd pictured endless days together, playing and making love. A sweet repeat of those holidays spent in the Vineyard.

That last summer before she'd turned fifteen had been magical, despite the secret they'd been keeping. Or maybe because of it. She'd earned his undivided attention, and she craved that same connection now, but he was too wrapped up in his medical studies to give her the attention she desired. Every day she reminded herself that this period in their lives wouldn't last forever.

She worked her way across the bar and slid into the booth with the other members of her class. Many had returned home for the summer, but the few left were hanging out more frequently. It felt like they were finally accepting her into the group even if it had taken a little encouragement from Derrick for her to join them.

"You're distracted." Annalise raised a brow. "Another fight with the ole ball 'n chain?"

Tiffany smirked, thinking about the passionate make-up sessions that followed their heated, fiery bursts of emotions. Their reconciliation last night had become off-the-charts scorching hot. It always was. "His name is Aiden."

"Ha. I knew it. Another fight followed by crazy make-up sex. Am I right?" Annalise asked.

She shrugged, fighting the smile twitching at the corner of her lips. The loud snort caught her attention. "What?"

"Nothing." Derrick smirked.

"Coward," Tiffany muttered.

"You two are always fighting." A sneer curled his lip. "You deserve better."

"Like it's any of your business?" Tiffany turned her back on the man, now wishing she stayed home.

"Hey. Don't be like that." His warm breath tickled her neck as he moved closer.

She tossed a scowl over her shoulder and wiggled out of the booth, scooping up her drink and heading to an empty seat she'd spotted at the bar. Derrick could be fun, and they'd been spending far more time together, but sometimes he acted like a complete jerk about her status as a married woman.

Moments later, the guy in question wiggled in between her and the woman on the next stool. "Sorry. Are you mad?"

She shrugged and sipped the icy peach Bellini.

Derrick slid a finger under her chin. "You know I'm right. It's like you spend half of your time fighting with him or making up with him." His sweet breath hit her cheek, and seconds later, his lips were on hers, his tongue caressing hers.

For a second she allowed it, soaking up the gentleness of his mouth. Thoughts of Aiden poured into her mind. *What am I doing?* She pressed a flattened palm against Derrick's chest and pushed him away, dropping her head and allowing a curtain of hair to fall over her burning face.

"Tiff?"

A small shudder coursed through her at the use of the shortened form of her name. Aiden was the only one allowed to call her that. She shook her head. "We can't do this. I love him."

He heaved a heavy sigh and stepped away, holding his hands up with his palms facing her. "You deserve so much more than him," he said before he wove his way toward the table.

The glare from Annalise didn't make Tiffany feel any better about the encounter. She had just kissed another man. She could never tell Aiden. He'd never forgive her, especially after their recent heated discussions over this very man.

She grabbed her bag and hurried toward the exit, knowing there was only one place she wanted to be right now. Half an hour later, she arrived at the hospital, waving at Matthias who had also scored a position in Philly for the summer.

"Looking for Aiden? He's helping one of the attending work up a patient, so he'll be a while."

"I just wanted to see him. I scarcely remember what he looks like." She offered a shy smile to her husband's friend, trying to hide the emotional upheaval going on inside.

"I'll tell him you're here." Matthias strode down the hallway.

A few moments later, Aiden appeared. "Everything okay, Tiff?" He leaned in and gave her a kiss, a frown appearing.

"What?" Tiffany pressed her fingertips to her lips.

"You taste different. Like a weird combination of peaches and orange liquor. You hate orange flavored drinks. What have you been into?"

"Nothing." She dipped her chin. "Just a Bellini. I was on my way home and thought I'd say hi. When will you be done?"

Aiden looked at his watch and blew out a long breath. "Three, maybe four hours. Sorry, we're slammed so I should get back." His eyes filled with concern as he studied her. "Are you okay? Something's wrong."

"I need some sleep." She stretched and widened her mouth in a fake yawn, pressing the back of her hand over her lips. "See you later?"

"I'll head home as soon as possible." He planted another kiss on her lips. "See you soon."

It surprised her that she had an aptitude for business, but she enjoyed the challenge her classes represented. Her husband had been right. They would be a valuable asset, especially when she realized her dream of owning a gallery. She knew it would happen someday. With Aiden's support and encouragement, it was inevitable.

Over the next months, Tiffany worked hard at remaining positive, though she spent much time alone. Even after school began in September, she concentrated on her art and work at the gallery.

Aiden was half-done with medical school, having entered his third year. She only had to hang on for a little while longer, and then they might be able to move back to Chicago. Philly wasn't and would never be home to her.

Her birthday passed much like the previous one, with her immersed in her work at the gallery and Aiden involved with his classes, study group, and labs. Christmas drew nearer, along with their second anniversary, and she began shopping for the holiday and preparing for a special night of celebration with her husband.

But it turned out their special day and the evening out she'd hoped for never happened due to his exams and studying schedule. She couldn't be upset with him as medical school had to come first, even on their anniversary. The day passed with no husband in sight, made only slightly better by the gorgeous display of roses that arrived at the door.

The next morning, Aiden rose early, kissed her lightly on the lips and rushed out the door. The final exam was scheduled to start at nine.

Another day alone. Her classes were done until after the holidays. She headed for their closet, digging into the bottom of the box of photos tucked away in the corner. As she pulled out the elaborately wrapped album she'd prepared for Aiden commemorating their marriage, a package of photos spilled onto the floor.

Tiffany kneeled, scooping them up and straightening them. One in particular caught her eye. One that brought back memories of happier times with her family. "Mom," she whispered, tracing a fingertip over the smiling faces.

They'd had traumatic, difficult times, and she wasn't sure she could forgive the cold treatment. Yet she couldn't shake the warm feelings that rose when she remembered her days as a young child. The hugs. The trips to the zoo and the beach. The bedtime stories. Maybe it was inevitable for a girl to miss her mother.

She trekked into the bedroom, sitting on the edge of the mattress and rubbing her hands over her denim-clad thighs before gathering the courage to dial. "Hi, Mom," she whispered when the soft feminine voice flowed down the line.

"Tiffany. Why are you calling?"

"I thought—"

"Are you ready to come home?"

"I hoped you might visit us before Christmas. Aiden and I would love to see you."

"Stubborn man," her mother said under her breath. "The only way your father will allow contact is if you divorce him. David will accept nothing less."

She straightened her spine and clutched the phone between her trembling fingers, sucking in a painful breath. *Leave Aiden?*

"He knows this." Michelle's voice dropped an octave. "You haven't left him have you?"

"No." Tiffany practically choked on the word. *Aiden knew?*

"I have to go. Your father just pulled into the garage but—"

As she blinked hard to quell the tears, Tiffany set the receiver into the cradle with a soft click. Her parents didn't love her enough to forgive her or allow her back into their lives. Her husband had lied. He'd told her it was nothing. Now she knew what Aiden had been keeping from her. *My entire family was gone unless I gave up my marriage.*

Anger flooded through her and she tossed everything into the container and shoved it into the corner. Worst of all, there was nothing she could do about it. Aiden was sequestered in a room at the university, taking a final exam, leaving her alone to deal with this devastating news.

She rifled through her clothing, picking out a pair of snug-fitting jeans before running a brush through her long locks. After adding a touch of make-up to highlight her blue eyes, she donned a set of high-heeled dress boots and headed for the door. Damned if she would sit around waiting for him, stewing over his lies and deceptions.

A few minutes later she arrived at the pub, smiling and waving as she joined the group gathered around one of the high tables.

"I didn't think you were coming." Derrick looped an arm around her shoulders and gave her a light squeeze. "You look fantastic."

She bestowed her brightest smile on her friend. "I need a drink."

"Coming right up." He flagged down a server and ordered two rounds of shots. "Keep 'em coming."

"Where's Annalise?" She scanned the surrounding area.

"She went home for the holidays. I leave on Thursday, as Gabe asked me to help with the two shows this week. How about you?"

"We'll be here." Tiffany tipped back another shot.

The alcohol coursed through Tiffany's system and she swayed to the beat of the music. This was exactly what she needed to forget what felt like a betrayal from both her mother and her husband.

"I thought you'd be heading to Chicago to celebrate with your family. But let me guess. Aiden's at work. Or at school. Or somewhere other than with his wife."

"Close. He's writing an exam." She took a long sip of her drink. "Yesterday was our anniversary. Two years of wedded bliss." A small scoff escaped.

"Sounds convincing." He shook his head. "What did you do?"

"Aiden studied with his group. I ate popcorn for dinner and watched a movie."

"That sucks." Derrick waved at the server to bring another round. "You'd think he'd make time for that at least."

She lifted a shoulder. "Doesn't much matter. There will be other anniversaries." A sniffle escaped and she dropped her head onto her forearms as the alcohol coursed through her system. Her head felt light and she knew she'd better slow down. She had a low tolerance.

"What's wrong?" He rubbed her back with a warm hand. "You seem unhappy."

"I should go home." Tiffany pushed to her feet, but swayed as her knees trembled, threatening to give way.

"Whoa." Derrick reached out and steadied her. "I'll take you." He grabbed her coat and held it out before leading her out the door.

Tiffany stepped into the quiet apartment. "Come in."

Derrick peered around. "Nice place."

"It's too big." She forced the lump from her throat as this new and unbidden thought raced through her mind. Though she'd never considered it before, for two people, one of whom was never home, there was far more space than needed. "Aiden isn't home all that often these days." Tiffany grabbed two sodas from the fridge, offering one to Derrick.

The guy lounged on the couch, looking comfortable in her living room. "So you keep telling me." His vivid blue eyes traveled over her, and he swept a hand through his wavy blond hair.

"There's no end in sight. Soon he'll start hospital rotations with shifts, so that should be fun." She sipped her drink, dropping down beside him. "Being a doctor's wife isn't exciting."

"Neglecting you, is he?"

Tiffany shrugged and looked away. "We've been married two years, and yesterday was our anniversary." She sighed. "He had a huge exam today so it wasn't romantic, but he promised to make it up to me."

"He should have done something for you. If you were my girl …"

Tiffany frowned, feeling disloyal for talking so openly with Derrick, but this man seemed to be her only friend these days. And the past few months had been difficult. She missed the early days when she'd moved to Philly and those magical first months of being newlyweds where they'd hardly kept their hands off of each other. Now with her at school all day, and Aiden often at study sessions or in class until late, it seemed like they barely connected at all, unless they were fighting or having make-up sex.

She sank onto the couch beside him and brushed at her burning eyes with her fingertips. "My parents feel the same." The words passed her alcohol-numbed lips before she could think better of it. "I've been told I can't come home until I give him up."

"I'm sorry."

His soft voice made her peek up at him. She froze in place, her heart pounding as he leaned closer.

Derrick bent his head and kissed her gently, pausing to peer into her eyes before their lips met again.

Her breath caught in her throat as he wrapped his arms around her, hugging her against his chest.

"Sorry," he whispered.

Tiffany rested her head against his chest, thinking how she missed these moments with Aiden. "I can't, I'm …" Her arms slipped around him and she reveled in the comfort.

"I know." He rocked her.

Lifting her head again was her biggest mistake. His lips crushed hers as he pressed his body against hers. The next few moments blurred in her mind as he caressed her breast through her sweater, the pressure of his mouth increasing as her hand drifted to the nape of his neck to play with the strands of his hair.

"Ah, Derrick." She pulled back and swiped her hand over her lips. "We can't."

Derrick stroked her cheek with his thumb. "I'm falling in love with you."

"No." She shook her head. "You can't." The harsh intake of breath rasped down her throat. Her head swam at his words, muddled and fuzzy. *The lies. The loneliness. The everything that I hoped for in my marriage that wasn't and may never be. Everything he'd promised and failed to deliver.*

Reality faded into a blur as Derrick's arms wrapped around her. Orange-tinged wisps of air wafted against her cheek before soft lips pressed against the soft flesh of her neck. Into that spot that drove her crazy.

Tiffany tipped her head as an involuntary moan escaped. The conflicting emotions rolled through her. She sighed as he dropped butterfly kisses across her shoulder, up her neck, not stopping until he captured her mouth. Desire flickered to life. It shocked and thrilled her that another man could make her feel this way. If she closed her eyes, she could pretend.

Fingers slid under her, lifting, and she wrapped her legs around him, sinking deeper into the kiss. In no time at all, they were sinking into the mattress, surrounded by the luxurious sheets she'd chosen.

They took their time undressing, clothing coming off slowly as Derrick kissed her and stroked her skin. It felt incredible, this entirely new and exciting experience. *The first time I've allowed anyone besides Aiden to touch me this way.* When Derrick moved over her, she welcomed him, wrapping her legs around him. She closed her eyes, digging her fingers into his back, knowing it was wrong, but overcome with emotions and desire. She was powerless to resist.

Chapter 15

Aiden

AIDEN SHIFTED THE FLORIST'S BOX to his other hand, and peeked into the bag, running over the gourmet meal in his mind as the elevator rose toward their suite.

Exams were finished and he'd handed over the flash drive with his part of the group project. The guys had understood his dilemma and promised they'd add his contribution and submit it for grading.

A pang of guilt nagged him for neglecting the single most important person in his life. Tonight he'd make it all up to her. After cooking her a gourmet dinner he'd unveil the surprise that would earn her forgiveness. The lost sleep and hours of study and planning would fade to nothing when he considered the joy this well-earned vacation would bring to the woman he loved.

The key slipped easily into the lock and he swung the door open, setting the over-flowing bags on the floor. His keys jingled in that familiar way as they hit the tray by the front door. He was about to set aside the flowers and peel off his sweatshirt and shoes when something struck him. The apartment wasn't silent as he'd expected. He froze, registering the sounds carrying down the stairs.

His hand clenched around the box as he moved forward, a cold sweat causing a shiver down his spine. Each step upward seemed an incredible, insurmountable effort, but he had to know. *Even if he didn't want to.*

His breath caught as he reached the bedroom door. The honey-blonde curls fanned across the pillow were unmistakeable. As were the sounds issuing from her throat. The long, slightly-too-thin pale legs wrapped around the guy twitched as another long moan issued from the direction of the bed. *Their bed.*

Nausea rose and a red-tinged haze descended over him. Aiden wasn't aware of making a sound, but anger flashed within him as he yanked the guy off the bed. He wrapped a hand around the offender's throat and brought his hand up even as his vision blurred.

"No." The shriek pierced the air a second too late.

Aiden's fist connected with the man's face with a sickening, but satisfying crunch, blood spurting onto the floor.

Fingers dug into his arm like eagle's talons. "Stop it."

"Get away." He shook her off and flexed his aching fingers.

His victim slid to the floor in a heap and clutched at his face as a groan escaped him. The guy seemed familiar but it was hard to tell with the man covering his features with his fingers and the blood gushing down his chin.

It didn't matter who. It only mattered that she had. Bruised roses and petals scattered as Aiden spun and stalked down the hallway.

"Wait." Her voice carried from behind him. "Don't leave. Please."

He didn't turn. His entire body quivered and rage clouded his vision as he bounded downstairs and snatched his keys from the tray the apartment door slamming behind him as he left. The stairwell door clanged against the wall as he shoved through it and charged down the steps two at a time, all the way to the parking garage.

"Fuck." He sank into the driver's seat of his car, pounding a fist on the steering wheel. After several deep breaths to stop his hands from shaking, he reversed out of his parking space and tapped on the steering wheel as the security door lifted. The tires squealed as he left the lot, grateful to have escaped. He had no idea where he was headed, but anywhere was better than here.

Somehow, he found his way to the turnpike, exiting onto I-95N. He brushed at his eyes, blinking away the furious tears as he hit the gas. The pictures flashed through his mind on repeat, and he flexed his left hand, his wedding ring digging into his finger.

As he held the steering wheel with one hand, he tugged at the band with two fingers of the other. He managed to work it as far as his knuckle before he grasped it between his teeth, wiggling it until it slid off. Air whistled through the car as he lowered the glass and flung the offending bit of gold out the window without a second glance.

The call display on his phone lit up as it chimed out the special ringtone. *Her ringtone.* An inescapable ache built and built, and he smacked his hand against the wheel, grimacing as pain shot from his bruised knuckles into his wrist. As he sped down the interstate, his phone continued to bleat periodically. *Damn phone wouldn't shut up. Her again?*

Threads of nausea curled in his stomach, almost overwhelming him. Even the icy air from the open window didn't help, and Aiden swerved onto the shoulder and slammed on the brakes. He lunged from the driver's seat, barely making it around the front hood before he heaved his stomach contents onto the ice-covered gravel, one hand pressed against the fender to steady him. Blasts of freezing air from the traffic rushing by slammed him, making his eyes sting and water. His knees shook and threatened to buckle as he dragged air into his burning lungs.

After several deep breaths, he wobbled the final few feet to the passenger door and sank onto the seat, dropping his head into his hands. The phone vibrated in the console where he'd left it. *Tiffany, again.* Aiden clenched it in his hand, staring without truly seeing as the message notification chimed. It buzzed again, her name taunting him from the lit screen. "Fuck you." The phone flew from his fingers as he rose and launched it into the field. The device disappeared into the gloom of settling dusk. *Everything I ever believed to be true disappeared.*

With a smothered sob, he bowed his head, his shoulders sagging. His legs refused to move. He had nowhere to go anyway. No home. No family. Without Tiffany, there was nothing left.

The occasional wash of headlights fell over him as cars continued to speed by. Eventually, he swept a hand over his damp cheeks and rounded the car, sliding into the driver's seat and resting his head on the steering wheel. Numbness crept through his body, his mind functioning on auto-pilot as he managed several shaky breaths and started the engine, merging into traffic.

The road blurred and time passed by, yet he had no idea where he was headed or what he'd do once he arrived. Then a sign illuminated by the beam of his headlights caught his eye. *Lincoln Tunnel?* He veered off of the interstate and exited. *New York might be just what I needed.* Manhattan was the ideal place to lose himself in the bustling crowd.

Once through the tunnel, he watched for a familiar hotel, and pulled up to the valet. He arrived at the check-in counter, reeling with exhaustion. At the clerk's request, he presented his credit card and answered the standard questions.

"Welcome back, Mr. Hamilton. Can I have a bellman assist with ...?" A frown settled on the clerk's face as he peered over the counter. "No bags, sir?"

"I ..." Aiden glanced down, realizing he had nothing but the clothes on his back. He certainly couldn't face explaining how and why he came to be standing in a luxury hotel without so much as a toothbrush. This young man wouldn't care anyway. "They lost my luggage."

"I'm sorry, but it happens all the time. There's a boutique if you need attire." The clerk pointed across the lobby. "I'll notify housekeeping to provide a complimentary basket of essentials."

Aiden accepted his room keys and thanked the desk clerk before wandering into the small store. He selected several clothing items along with a jacket and dropped them onto the counter.

"Lost suitcase?" The clerk eyed the pile.

Aiden nodded. "Damn airlines."

"It's half our business." The young woman smiled as she held out the shopping bag. "Have a good night, sir."

Aiden rode the elevator to his floor, easily locating his room. After kicking off his shoes, he flopped across the massive bed and shielded his eyes with the back of his hand. "How could you?" he muttered under his breath.

The pain of betrayal raced through him all over again. He'd loved her forever, and she'd repaid him this way? The violation of trust and betrayal gutted him.

His feet hit the floor and he stomped to the minibar. The contents weren't fancy, but they'd do. In a quick motion, he twisted the cap off one of the tiny liquor bottles and poured the contents down his throat.

The burn made his eyes water, but he lobbed the empty toward the trash bin and dug several more airline-sized containers from the bar. The bright lights of the busy streets below enticed him to the window. As he stared over the city, he drained each bottle. The vibrant vista below beckoned, inviting him to come out and play.

"Hell ya." He emptied the final bottle before he dumped the contents of his shopping bag onto the bed. In a matter of ten minutes, he'd changed and pulled on the leather jacket he'd purchased in the boutique.

After a cursory glance at his reflection, he left the room, slamming the door behind him.

Aiden sighed as he scanned the queue for the nightclub. New York was infamous for its lines, and he had no option but to wait. He shoved his hands into his coat pockets, wishing he'd chosen something warmer. Fluffy snowflakes drifted around him as he shuffled his feet. The happy chatter of the surrounding groups made him feel even more alone, but he didn't have the energy to join in or start up a conversation.

"Hi, honey."

Aiden looked up at the touch on his arm, meeting the amber eyes of a beautiful dark-haired woman.

"Hi." His gaze was drawn downward over her shapely legs, landing on the sexy stiletto heels before rising to her face.

"I haven't seen you before. I'd remember." Her eyebrows rose, her lips twitching. "I'm Angelica."

"Aiden."

"How are you getting in? Are you on the list?"

"No." Aiden offered her a faint smile. "Do I need to be?"

"Not if you're with me." She linked her arm through his and pulled him out of the line, leading him past the crowd to the front door.

"Good evening, Ms. Giannelli." The bouncer nodded and unhooked the rope, waving them through with barely a glance at Aiden.

"See? No problem." Angelica ran a hand down his arm and blinked at him slowly. "Shall we?"

He followed as she swayed across the room and slid into a booth marked 'reserved.' "Can I buy you a drink?"

"It's on me. I run a tab."

Aiden nodded as a server appeared and set them up with a round of shots. This had turned out better than expected. He'd assumed he'd stand in line for hours, even if he was fairly certain he wouldn't drink alone. He never did.

"So, Aiden. Tell me about yourself." Angelica ran her fingertips across his hand, stopping on the faint indent and pale line on his ring finger. "Are you married?"

"Separated."

"I'm sorry to hear that." Angelica studied his face. "I'm divorced."

"I'm sorry."

"Don't be. Would you like to dance?"

Several hours and countless drinks later, Aiden had forgotten his afternoon, or almost … This escape was what he'd needed. A release from the endless pain. He longed to erase the picture of his traitorous wife's ring glinting mockingly at him as she moaned in pleasure … into another man's ear.

Angelica brushed a hand up the side of his face, caressing with her fingertips. Her luscious red lips parted, and she licked them in invitation. "Okay, baby?" As he nodded, she wrapped her hand around the back of his neck, applying a gentle pressure to bring him in for a kiss.

At the touch of her lips, he closed his eyes and sank into her embrace. *Why the hell should I remain faithful?* He hadn't lied to Angelica. The official separation had started the moment he'd found his wife's legs wrapped around another man. His gold leash had been discarded somewhere along I-95 and he felt liberated.

He opened his eyes and gazed down into the woman's glittering amber orbs. It would be so easy to lose himself in the atmosphere of this club and soak up the attentions of the undeniably sexy vixen in his arms.

Angelica swayed alluringly, pressing her sinuous body into his. She had him entranced, and he refused to fight the desire that grew within him. *Gorgeous.* The word popped into his mind as he grazed his fingers over her hips, drawing her closer. The warmth of Angelica's touch enticed him, their bodies molding together as they gyrated to the beat of the bass. Her soft hands covered his, guiding them over her body as she rubbed that perfect round ass against him.

Her beguiling scent wafted around him as she lifted her chin and whispered against his ear, "I need a drink." Linking their fingers, she tugged him toward the booth.

Aiden waved at the server before angling his head to stare into her eyes. The length of her leg pressed against his, while her hand caressed his thigh, creeping upward with each stroke. At the sight of her tongue darting out to lick those full lips, he leaned in and nipped at the bottom one before devouring her mouth with his own. Desire rose unchecked as he wrapped his hand in her silky hair. "Last round?" he murmured before capturing her mouth for another kiss.

She tipped up her chin. "Where are you staying?" Angelica ran a hand up his thigh, squeezing gently.

"The Park Hyatt." He nodded at the server, handing Angelica her drink before tipping back his own glass.

"Sounds delightful." She stood, offering her hand.

Aiden slid his hand into hers. The invitation in her eyes was clear and he was all in.

They'd barely stepped inside his room before Angelica had her arms around him. Aiden pressed her against the wall, kissing her as he slid his fingers under the straps of her silky dress. It slithered into a pool on the floor around her feet.

They exchanged fierce kisses as she tackled the buttons on his shirt. Moments later, her fingertips were stroking his bare chest and Aiden dropped his shirt to the floor.

Aiden buried his face into her hair, inhaling deeply and nuzzling her neck as he unhooked her bra.

"Mmm." A soft sigh emitted from her mouth as his lips brushed the nape of her neck. Angelica cupped a hand against his face, while the other wandered down to tug at his belt and pluck at the button on his pants.

Without missing a beat, he backed her toward the massive bed, enjoying the rising heat of her satiny skin. As he tipped her onto the bed, he divested her of the skimpy, lacy, sexy thong in one smooth motion. He gazed down at the beautiful naked woman on his bed for a moment before he removed the last of his clothing and joined her.

The woman bit her lip, running her hands over his biceps and into his hair as he nibbled at the sensitive spots on her neck. "Condom. In my bag," she whispered. She wiggled off the bed, strutting over to scoop her clutch from the floor near the door. A smile touched her lips as she retrieved a handful of small square packages and tossed all but one onto the nightstand.

"An optimist." Aiden bit back a laugh.

"I have faith in you, honey." She winked.

Aiden flipped back the covers and snaked an arm around her waist. Moments later, he had Angelica spread across the bed as he kissed her hot smooth skin and stroked her magnificent body. He captured her lips and took the presented packet from her fingertips and ripped it open.

Angelica slid her fingertips down his back and over his ass, pulling him to her. Her warm breath fanned against his skin as she sighed against his lips and curled a leg around his hip. Her small gasps became soft moans.

Aiden caressed her mouth with his, savoring the sweet aftertaste of orange liqueur on her tongue. He buried his head against her neck and tried to enjoy the sensations sweeping through him, but still, an unbidden thought crept in. *Now we were even.*

"Aiden?" Angelica's soft hands cupped his cheeks, the questioning look in her eyes forcing him to refocus on what was happening, here and now.

The end of everything I treasured.

He smothered her next words with a deep kiss, gratified with her response. A soft moan left her lips and her fingernails dug into his back as he returned his attention to the incredible woman in his arms. At this moment, nobody else and nothing else mattered.

⁓

Aiden awoke, unsure of where he was and with who, but then the memories rushed in. The warmth of Angelica's naked body against his as she nestled in his arms. Her enticing womanly scent and satiny skin. He loathed leaving the comfort of the bed, but he stretched and he peeled himself away, heading toward the minibar in search of a bottle of water.

The cap made a small cracking sound as he broke the seal and gulped down several mouthfuls while on his way to the bed. He dropped into the tangle of sheets, noting the bright amber eyes peering at him from under half-opened lids. With a smile, he offered her the bottle.

"Thanks." She propped herself on one elbow before sipping the icy water. "I haven't slept that soundly in ages."

Aiden contemplated the woman as he tucked a hand behind his head and reclined against his pillow. "What keeps you up at night?"

"What doesn't?" Angelica combined the slightest lift of her shoulder with the tiniest of smirks. "You get to a certain age and the stresses of life tend to wear on you."

He contained his grin. "Surely you aren't that old," he said.

"I'm thirty-three." Her nose wrinkled. "The old divorced lady picking up sweet young things at the club. Some would label me a cougar." A soft snicker left her lips. "I'm scared to ask how old you are, honey. Twenty-four? Twenty-five?"

"Close enough," he said. No way would he admit he was still several months shy of the legal drinking age. This woman would run for the door if she knew, and he found her company enjoyable. Aiden twirled a lock of her dark silky hair around his fingertip, planting a tender kiss on her lush lips. "Stay," he murmured.

She caught his left hand in hers. "Nobody expecting you home?" Her perfect brow arched as her gaze rested on the ring of untanned flesh on his finger. "I'll probably go to hell for sleeping with a married man."

"You're in no danger." Aiden trickled his fingertips along her hip. If anyone deserved the fiery pit, it was his treacherous, cheating wife. His lips twisted as he pictured the scene from the day before and his abandoned plans. "Anyone expecting you home?"

"No." She tilted her head. "Are you sure about your nobody? That expression says otherwise."

He lifted a shoulder. "If she's expecting me home, she's delusional."

"So it's like that." Angelica's gripped his hand. "I'm sorry, Aiden," she said softly. "I've been there." She grazed her fingers down his chest. "I'd like to stay," she murmured, her eyes holding a world of promise.

Aiden captured her lips, winding an arm around her as he pulled her down amongst the tangled sheets, grateful for the distraction, but mostly happy he wasn't alone with his thoughts.

Chapter 16
Tiffany

RING. PLEASE, PLEASE. RING. TIFFANY fixated her red, puffy eyes on the phone, combing her shaking fingers through her hair. Three long excruciating days had passed, and she hadn't heard a single word.

She couldn't sleep or eat and had barely moved from this spot except to pace and wear a track in the floor. *Where had he gone? Would he ever forgive my transgression?*

"Please, please call me," she whispered, clutching her phone to her chest.

Aiden wasn't with Will, Ben, or Matthias. After he'd missed their study session on Friday, Will called her. She lied and said he'd come down with the flu. The follow-up calls inquiring about her husband's health assured her that his friends didn't know the situation, but also caused a frisson of panic as she realized Aiden had disappeared.

She dragged herself to her feet and pressed the phone to her ear.

The mailbox is full. Please—

A scream of frustration burst from her lips, and she hurled her phone onto the sofa. She buried her face in her hands but brought her head up as her mobile rang. A mad rush across the room had the device within reach, and she snatched it up. "Aiden?"

"No. It's Tom," the deep male voice said, the concern evident in his tone. "Aiden's not returning my calls, which is unlike him. Where is he?"

Tiffany bowed her head and sniffled.

"Tiffany?" Tom's voice grew stern. "Put Aiden on the phone."

"I …" She hiccuped out a sob.

"Where is he?"

"I don't know. He left me."

"He what?" Tom asked. "What happened? When did he leave?"

"Thursday," she whispered.

"You haven't heard from your husband in three fucking days, and you didn't call me?"

"I thought he'd come home." She closed her eyes. "How could I call you? You're his friend."

"Exactly. That's the reason you should have called. Has anyone heard from him? What about the guys there?"

She nibbled at a fingernail. "They don't know he left."

"Bloody hell, Tiffany. Why did he leave in the first place?" Tom's voice dropped. "This wasn't a simple disagreement or he'd be back. Spit it out."

"I can't."

"Yes, you can. And you will, damn it. He's never gone this long without returning calls and now his voice mail is full, and you have no idea where he is, so he must be in serious trouble."

"Just find him. Please?" Tiffany dropped her chin to her chest, picking at a loose thread on her sweater and tugging at it, staring as it unraveled. "He won't call me back."

"Did he take his car? Any clothes?"

"His car is gone." That had been one of the first things she'd checked. The wild pursuit down the stairs after she'd come to her senses had revealed the empty parking space.

The line went dead. She pulled up her knees, wrapping her arms around them and rocking to calm herself, fixing her gaze on the crystal vase in the middle of the coffee table. The roses from the florist's box, their petals bruised and squished and several stems sticking out at odd angles were damaged beyond repair. She feared her marriage would meet a similar fate.

Those moments after Aiden had stormed out were a hazy memory. Derrick hurling insults, cursing at her as he mopped the blood from his face with one of the fluffy bathroom towels. *Slut. Bitch. You'll pay for this!* But the words bounced off, nothing but fragments and white noise as she'd scrambled to rescue the bent, crushed stems and cradled them against her chest, mindless of the scratches on her forearms and the tears dripping from the end of her nose. *Twenty-four. Two dozen formerly flawless, deep red roses.*

What she'd done was stupid. Her moment of weakness, her fleeting desire for comfort, destroyed everything. *How would Aiden ever forgive me?* She curled into a ball on the end of the couch, sobbing as she wrapped her arms around herself.

After what might have been hours, or even minutes later, pounding on the door woke her. The room had dimmed, a sign the afternoon had worn on. Dark dreary clouds had rolled in and icy flecks of snow clicked against the window. Tiffany dragged herself from the couch and cracked open the door.

Will pushed past her into the apartment, followed by Ben. "What's going on?"

She stared at her feet and shook her head. *How could I look at him?* The guilt must be written all over her face.

"Tom called me." Will grasped her shoulders and shook her. "Aiden's been gone for days. Why did you say he was sick?"

"I thought he'd be back. He always comes back to me."

"Ben and I have searched for hours and visited every place we could think of." Will led her to the sofa and forced her to sit, kneeling in front of her. "Talk to me. Tell me everything. Do you know where he might go?"

"No." She shook her head. "Last time I saw him was Thursday at around three in the afternoon. I thought he'd be studying, but he came home early." Her cheeks flushed as she rubbed her hands over her face, avoiding Will's gaze.

"And then what?"

A shiver ran through her and she curled into a ball. She hadn't meant for it to happen. Aiden had been the love of her life for so long, and now …

"Nothing," she whispered. "We had a fight and he took off."

"You're lying. Where did he go?"

"I don't know."

"Did he pack anything?"

"No."

Will pulled out his phone. "Tom? We're at Aiden's apartment. There's no sign of him anywhere." He paced back and forth and scrubbed a hand through his hair. "They traced his phone?"

She lifted her head, her breath catching at the alarmed expression on Will's face.

Will sank onto the chair across from her, bowing his head. "I'll tell her." He hung up and lifted his gaze. "They found his phone in a field alongside I-95, ten miles from Philadelphia. There's no sign of Aiden."

A crushing force on her chest made it difficult to breathe, and she gasped for air. She'd been sitting here for days, thinking he'd show up and calling that stupid phone every five minutes. Blackness descended.

"Tiffany?" A hand patted her cheek. "Wake up."

She opened her eyes slowly, hoping the past days had all been a bad dream. When she met the concerned gaze of Ben, she knew it was all too real.

"Are you with us?" He helped her sit, pressing a glass of water into her trembling hands.

"Is he …?" Her trembling voice locked up in her throat. She simply couldn't utter the words.

"Tom's tracking credit card usage. If Aiden's done anything like purchase gas, stayed in a motel, or charged a meal, we'll know." Will's face came into focus as he appeared beside Ben. "We won't give up until we find him."

"What if we don't find him? What if something happened?" Her chest burned, and she longed to retreat into blackness. "What if he's …?"

"Don't think like that. Is there anyone who can stay with you? We need to be out looking for Aiden." Ben patted her hand. "You should stay here in case he comes home."

Tiffany shook her head. "I'll be okay. Find him, please? I need him." She twirled a chunk of hair around her finger and tugged on it.

Will narrowed his eyes and headed toward the stairs, bounding up them two at a time.

"He's not up there," she said. The sound of cabinets slamming greeted her ears followed by the reverberation of footsteps.

"Are you hurt?" Will lifted her chin with a finger, examining her closely. "There's blood all over the floor and wall, and bloody towels in the sink." His eyes widened. "Is he okay, Tiffany? Is that his blood?"

"What?" Ben dashed for the stairs.

She shook her head. "It's not his. I didn't …" The tears broke free, flooding down her raw cheeks and making her eyes burn. "I'd never hurt him. How could you ever think I'd do that?"

"I've heard you two fight, that's how," he muttered. "It's clearly not yours, and you say it's not his, so who's is it?"

Her shoulders sagged, and she buried her face in her hands.

Will blew out a stream of air. "Wow. You faithless little bitch." He pushed to his feet. "Is there a dead body around we should worry about?"

Ben reappeared, holding what appeared to be credit card statements. "I'll make sure Tom has both of the numbers. It might be time for a police report."

"Police?" Tiffany's head bobbed as a shudder ran through her. "Why the police?"

"He's been gone for days. Call us right away if you hear from him. And get someone to come stay with you." Ben's voice sounded icy and distant. "There's nothing here to tell us where he's gone, so let's get a report filed and then go out there and keep looking."

"No police." Will shook his head. "Tom is on it, and I know he has connections. I don't think we need to get anyone else involved just yet. He'll check all the hospitals and make some discreet inquiries."

A few minutes later, Tiffany was alone again, helpless and desperate to know what to do next. *Nothing.* If Tom couldn't find him, nobody would. "Please come home," she whispered. "I love you, Aiden. Please forgive me." She slumped onto the couch, pressing her phone against her chest, willing it to ring. Wishing for him to come home and pleading for the chance to take it all back.

Chapter 17

Aiden

Soft lips touched Aiden's temple. "I have to go," Angelica whispered against his ear. "My car is waiting."

He rolled and gazed up at her. "London calling, right?"

"If I could skip the meeting, I would." She perched on the side of the bed and stroked his cheek with her fingertips. "My card is on the table. Anytime you're in New York, look me up. I mean it, Aiden."

"I promise." Aiden cupped her cheek with his palm and drew her down for a last kiss. "Bye, Angie."

After gracing him with a gentle smile, she disappeared out the door. Aiden dropped his hand over his eyes. He'd enjoyed every minute of this amazing woman's company over the weekend. Though she'd attended meetings at her Manhattan office on Friday, she'd joined him Friday evening, and they'd spent Saturday together lounging in bed and ordering room service. Now the first light of Sunday morning crept into the room.

The hurt and pain he'd locked away for the past three days rose up with a vengeance. Tiffany had cruelly ripped his heart out. *How had I not seen it coming?*

He curled up in the massive bed, drifting in a twilight haze. Hours later, he woke up again and crawled from the bed, rummaging in the mini bar and coming up empty. He lacked the energy to shower and dress, and it was too early to bother. Nothing would be open this early on a Sunday. At least nowhere he wanted to go. He dialed room service and ordered a burger and two bottles of Macallan.

―⚔―

Aiden batted at the hand on his shoulder. "Fuck off." His head pounded, threatening to split wide open, and his tongue felt swollen, pasty, and dry.

"Is that anyway to speak to your best friend?" The familiar voice nagged at him. "Hey. Look at me."

"Go away," he muttered and buried his head under the pillow.

"Nope. Open your eyes."

He rolled, cracking one eye open and peering out from under the puffy lid. "What are you doing here?"

Tom sat on the side of the bed and pressed a bottle of water into Aiden's hand. "Drink."

"Already did." His eyelid drooped shut and he tried to turn over.

"I can see that, which is why you need water." Tom shook him again. "Open your eyes and drink."

"Not buggering off?"

"So you disappear again? Not a chance. Why didn't you call me?" Tom prodded Aiden in the ribs. "Drink."

"Dunno." He wiggled into a sitting position and sipped from the bottle, eyeing Tom warily.

"More." His friend tipped the bottle against Aiden's lips and shook two tablets into his hand. "Take these. Your head must be pounding. You look like shit and smell worse. I'll warm up the shower." He disappeared into the bathroom.

Aiden didn't answer, but he popped the pain relievers into his mouth, washing them down with another swig of water. He closed his eyes and rubbed the back of his neck hoping to ease the thud in his temples.

Tom reappeared. "Up." He yanked back the covers and hauled Aiden from the bed, dragging him into the bathroom. He pointed at the running shower. "Get in. I'll sort this mess. Housekeeping would be disgusted, and that's saying something."

Aiden leaned a hand against the tile of the stall, grateful for the hot water sluicing over him. Deep breaths did nothing to calm the roll of his stomach and he lurched out of the stall, hung over the toilet, and heaved. He cursed the fact that he hadn't done anything but drink in recent memory. Everything ached and his throat burned.

"You okay?" Tom asked from behind him.

"Fine." He waved before running the back of his hand over his mouth.

"Good. Finish your shower. Then you can cover that bare ass."

Aiden stumbled into the shower again and dumped a liberal blob of shampoo into his hand. After scrubbing down, he slung a towel around his hips, rubbing at the mirror to clear a spot. He peered at his red-rimmed eyes and rough stubble, scratching at his chin. It surprised him that Angelica had stuck around as long as she had. He looked like a scruffy homeless man who'd snuck into a high-end hotel.

"You need this." Tom appeared again, slapping a razor and shaving cream onto the counter. "Is it safe to leave you unattended with sharp objects?"

"Ha, funny guy," Aiden glowered at Tom. "Go about your business."

"That could take hours. This place …." Tom strode out.

"Leave it." Aiden grimaced at the echo of his own voice in the bathroom.

"What?" Tom reappeared in the doorway, dangling a slip of lace between his thumb and forefinger.

"Just forget the mess. I'll provide a huge tip for the housekeepers."

"Yeah … no." Tom shook his head. "Your hotel room can't look like this. You know what the paparazzi is like, and the staff here knows your family." He extended his hand, waving the slinky black thong. "And who might this belong to?" His brows rose and his eyes widened. "La Perla?"

Aiden glowered as he squeezed toothpaste onto the toothbrush. The cottony texture in his mouth made him wonder if he'd chewed on his pillow.

Tom squinted and dropped the offending panties into the garbage. He made a show of washing his hands before he turned away, shaking his head as he left the bathroom.

The sounds of empty bottles clanking together and the thud of them landing in the trashcan made Aiden cringe and rub his temples.

"Good boy. You used protection, given the number of empty condom wrappers." Tom appeared at the bathroom door again.

"Fuck off," Aiden mumbled through a mouthful of toothpaste. "She wasn't a hooker."

"Yeah, I put that together. But you could show a little gratitude, asshole. I tracked you for three days."

Aiden rolled his eyes as he rinsed his mouth and ran a brush through his hair. After inspecting himself in the mirror, he shuffled into the main room.

"There are clean clothes on the bed." Tom held a business card in the air. "Angelica Giannelli, Vice-President, Acquisitions. A lawyer?"

Aiden yanked on the jeans and sweater and dropped onto the bed to pull on fresh socks. "Someone else could have left that."

"I've concluded the party in question is the owner of a sexy and expensive black lace thong. She left incontrovertible evidence." Tom retrieved the notepad from the desk and cleared his throat. *"Aiden, I had a great time."* Tom smirked. "I just bet she did. She left an invitation." He waved the note. *"Next time you're in New York, look me up. All my love, Angelica.* Don't lie, my friend. Especially not to someone studying evidentiary procedures."

"Stellar skills of deduction, counsellor."

"Sass. You're feeling better." Tom leveled his gaze at Aiden. "What the hell are you doing? Did you conveniently forget your wedding vows?"

Aiden dropped his head into his hands. A clear picture of that afternoon rushed in, forcing the breath from his lungs like he'd been sucker punched. He'd been a clueless idiot for marrying Tiffany so now Tom could claim his victory.

"Hey." Tom sank onto the bed beside him. "What happened?"

Aiden shook his head, hauling in a long breath as his throat closed up.

"It's bad, right?" Tom slid an arm around his shoulders. "I'm sorry about giving you a hard time, but you scared the living shit out of me. Don't ever disappear like that again."

Aiden rubbed a hand over his face, sucking in air while fighting the urge to crawl under the covers. Disappearing from the world seemed the kindest option, followed closely by his wish for death.

"We'll talk later. Let's get you home."

Tears burned his eyes, and his stomach rolled at the thought of facing the woman who'd annihilated him, shredded his heart, and broken his spirit, leaving him a quivering, needy mess. The words stuck in his throat but he said them anyway. "I no longer have a home."

His friend's brow furrowed. "Then you'll stay with me in New Haven for a bit. You have your car, right?"

Aiden nodded, still unable to look up.

"Why don't I order coffee and a light breakfast? You need something in your stomach before we get in the car."

"Okay," Aiden whispered.

Tom patted his shoulder, picking up the phone while Aiden crawled onto the bed and closed his eyes, grateful his friend had refrained from voicing the gloating words.

An hour later they were on the road toward New Haven. Aiden slumped in the passenger seat of his own car, propped against the window with his eyes closed. The coffee and triangle of toast he'd forced down at Tom's insistence had done little to settle the waves of nausea. All Aiden wanted to do was sink into unconsciousness and forget his messed-up life.

He felt the glances from Tom, but he pretended to sleep until his mouth watered, taking on a sour taste. "Pull over."

Tom didn't respond but he pulled the car to the side of the road.

Aiden flung open the passenger door and leaned out to vomit onto the gravel. He heaved endlessly, his eyes watering as his stomach rebelled. Once he was done, he accepted the water bottle Tom pressed into his hands and swished a mouthful around before spitting it onto the ground. He yanked the door closed and rested his forehead against the cold glass.

"Okay?" Tom asked.

At Aiden's small nod, Tom merged into traffic.

After several minutes of silence, his friend asked, "Want to talk about it?"

Aiden shook his head, turning away so Tom wouldn't see how close he was to a complete breakdown. Showing his emotions didn't come easily. His parents had never cared, and his grandfather had no patience for whining or crying, especially coming from young boys. So, he pushed it deep down inside, locking it away where it belonged.

"We're here." Tom's voice roused Aiden from his reverie.

"What?" Aiden blinked and squinted at the bright light assaulting his eyeballs.

"We'll be at my place in two minutes. Time to wake up."

"Oh." He rubbed at his tired, gritty eyes.

"Did you want to stop for some food?"

Aiden's stomach twisted at the thought. "I'm not hungry."

"You need to eat." Tom sighed. "You're a complete mess," he said as they descended into the underground parking. "Wait here while I grab the visitor tag from my car."

Aiden leaned against the door with his eyes closed until Tom returned and hung the parking pass on his mirror.

"I'm not planning to carry you." Tom's brow lifted.

Aiden slid out of the car and trailed after Tom to the elevators. The minute they were inside the cozy apartment, he sank onto the couch, curled up, and closed his eyes. He had nothing left. All that remained was a hollow empty shell. Shivers ran through him, he couldn't prevent the shake of his body. Aiden curled up tighter as the light weight of a blanket dropped over him.

"I'm grabbing food. I'll be back in ten minutes."

It seemed like only seconds later, and Tom prodded him. "I brought you soup."

Aiden clutched the blanket and shook his head.

"Eat. Do it yourself, or I will force-feed it to you. I suspect you haven't eaten in days." Tom shook him. "Sit up and eat, damn it."

Aiden forced himself upright and stared into the steaming bowl of chicken noodle soup on the coffee table in front of him. Noting the grim expression on his friend's face, he accepted a spoon. He had no doubt Tom would pour it down his throat if he didn't comply.

"Eat." Tom narrowed his eyes.

Aiden scooped a small spoonful into his mouth and swallowed hard. His stomach growled.

"Another one." Tom crossed his arms.

He managed another five spoonfuls under the watchful eye of his friend before he gave up, slumping against the back of the couch.

"You have to talk sometime. What happened with Tiffany?"

"She …" Aiden dragged in a long breath. "I came home, and she was …" A lump formed in his throat, making it impossible to utter the words.

"Holy hell." Tom's eyes widened. "She didn't!"

"She fucked some guy in our bed."

"I'm sorry." Tom squeezed Aiden's shoulder. "No wonder she acted so cagey. How long was it going on?"

"No idea." Aiden rubbed a hand through his hair. "Does it matter? Happy fucking anniversary to me."

"Shit. That was last week."

"Damn. What day is it?" He tried to sort the days in his mind, but everything remained a blur.

"Tuesday." Tom's brow rose. "We found your phone along the interstate on Sunday." His friend rested his forearms on his thighs. "Why didn't you call me?"

Aiden shrugged. "I don't expect anyone else to solve my problems." *And I didn't want to hear the "I told you so."*

"But it's me. You're my brother. If anything happened to you, it would kill me. Never scare me like that again."

"I'm sorry, I wasn't thinking straight. Or maybe I wasn't thinking at all. I'd just had a dagger driven straight through my heart. How could she fucking do that? In our home. In our bed." He pinched the bridge of his nose. "It's this horrible nightmare that won't stop playing in my head."

Tom closed his eyes and tipped his head downward. "I can only imagine how much this hurts. I'm sorry she did that."

"At least someone cares. My wife obviously doesn't."

"Well, either she's a great actress, or she cares deeply. Will and Ben have been checking in on her, and she's not looking so good."

"Yeah, her meal ticket found out she's a conniving, cheating bitch and left her. Must be stressful for the little princess. She played me good. Great actress is my vote."

"I don't think you believe that, Aiden. You've known her forever."

"Except I don't know her at all. And I'm done trying."

"So now what?"

"I'll find somewhere else to live until the end of the year and file for divorce."

"So no counseling or anything?"

"No. We're finished." Aiden closed his eyes.

"You don't want the apartment?"

"After that? No thanks. I'd torch the damn bed. I don't want to set foot in that place or see her face, ever again."

"You should make those decisions once you've had a chance to cool off." Tom observed him for several seconds. "The bed in the spare room is made up. Get some rest."

Aiden rose and dragged himself to the bedroom. He barely managed to strip off his clothes and climb under the covers and he was asleep.

Chapter 18
Tiffany

Tiffany clutched her phone to her chest and paced the room yet again. It was now late Tuesday night, and she hadn't heard a word. Her eyes were gritty and tired, and her hair hung in stringy clumps. She'd been scared to shower in case someone phoned.

Why did I do that? She asked herself the same question for at least the hundredth time as she stared out at the city lights. *What if something bad happened to Aiden?* Panic rose every time she thought of Tom finding his phone. Aiden had vanished without a trace. *Where would he go?*

If he'd shown up at one of his friend's homes, they'd have notified Tom. And Aiden would never go to Chicago, of that she was certain. All she could do was wait for news.

Regret ate at her. Derrick hadn't meant a damn thing, so why had she brought him home? *Why? Why?* She struggled for breath as she sank onto the couch and combed a hand through her straggly hair.

The interlude with Derrick hadn't been premeditated. Far from it. Even though they'd flirted, she'd never thought of her classmate in those terms. Besides, she loved Aiden. She'd waited for three years for him to come home. And now she'd ruined it and descended into a fog from which she might never emerge.

Unable to wait another second, she dialed. "Tom?" She twirled a strand of her hair around her finger, yanking hard. "Please tell me you found him. Tell me I haven't lost him forever."

"He's with me."

"Is he okay?"

"It depends on how you define okay." Tom's voice sounded flat to her ears. "Physically, he's in one piece. Emotionally, I'm not so sure."

"He told you? Or was it Will?" Her heart sank as she realized what this meant. Now it was inevitable that all of their friends would know what she'd done. It was only a matter of time before the news of her infidelity raced through the group. "Let me talk to him. Please?"

"He's sleeping."

"Wake him up. I need to—"

"No. There's nothing to be said right now."

"I'll come there. I can't sit around waiting for him to come home."

"Aiden doesn't want to talk to you. Stay away."

She choked back the sob as tears cascaded down her face. "Please," she whispered. "Tell him I'm sorry."

"I'm not your messenger. Back the fuck off and give the man some space. He'll contact you when he's ready. Until then, leave it alone."

With her fingers pressed to her mouth, she swallowed hard to combat her rising nausea. She didn't want to believe Tom's words. "I need him to come back. I need to explain."

"I doubt he's ready to hear it." Tom's voice softened only a touch. "Leave him be for a few days, Tiffany. I'll tell him you phoned. He's safe and in one piece. Let that be enough."

"Thank you."

The connection cut and she dropped her phone into her lap, staring at it silently. This had turned into a complete and utter mess. One stupid, tragic mistake and she ruined the best thing she'd ever had.

In the days that followed, the answer to her burning question became too obvious to miss. Aiden would never forgive her. She hadn't heard a single word from her husband's lips since the day he'd left her.

Tiffany dragged a hand through her lank hair and dialed Tom's mobile. "Is he there?"

"Not at the moment." Tom sighed. "Back off of him."

"How much further can I go?" she whispered. "I haven't spoken to him in over a week. Is he ever coming home?"

A heavy silence hung between them.

"He's never coming back?"

"I planned to call you later today," Tom said. "You need to leave the apartment for the afternoon so I can pack his stuff and have it moved."

The words stuck in her throat.

"You can live in the apartment for now. Once things settle, he'll contact you and the two of you can discuss what happens next."

"He's leaving me?" The anger grew inside her. "What a coward. He can't say it to my face? I don't even get to explain?"

"That's not my call. He asked me to retrieve his personal belongings," Tom said. "Can you vacate for a few hours?"

"He's in Philly?" The long silence spoke volumes, and she felt resigned to her fate. "I'll be gone in an hour."

"Thanks. I'll be as quick as possible."

Tiffany disconnected the call and flopped on the bed. Their future together had crumbled and it was all her fault. Nothing to do now but get out of the way. For a brief moment, she debated hanging around, but she didn't relish facing the wrath of Tom Grayson.

She dragged herself into the shower and dressed. Then she dug out the gifts she purchased for Christmas and tucked them into one of Aiden's bags. At the very least, he could open his presents. Maybe if he saw the love and care she'd put into choosing each item, he would understand how she felt about him.

She tugged the sweatshirt Aiden had left draped on the chair over her head before donning her scarf and wool coat. Her footsteps echoed hollowly in the hallway as she left the apartment. By the time she returned, her whole world would be unrecognizable.

It was after six by the time Tiffany unlocked the door and stepped inside the apartment. At first glance, it appeared that nothing had changed, except for the lingering silence and emptiness.

She took her time climbing the stairs. His laptop and books were gone from the office, but none of the furniture had been removed. Turning, she shuffled toward their room. She froze in the doorway, her eyes drawn to the colorful pile of boxes. The gifts she had so lovingly chosen and wrapped for Aiden had been dumped in the middle of their bed. *Our bed.* Except it wasn't *ours* any longer. It was hers alone.

Alone.

That single word took her legs from under her, and she crumpled to the floor, the tears stinging her cheeks as they broke free. Aiden had left her and might never come back. She'd cried for him when he'd disappeared from her life the year she'd turned fifteen. Except back then she'd had the hope he'd return to cling to. Now she had nothing. The chances of repairing her marriage was slim.

Eventually, her tears dried and she gathered the energy to look around. His bedside table had been cleared and a gaping hole had appeared in the closet.

A brightly colored ribbon peeking out of a bag on the floor under her dresses caught her eye, and she crawled across the wood toward it.

She extracted each parcel and laid them in a row. As she straightened the wedding ring set that still adorned her finger, she wondered if leaving them had been purposeful, or simply an oversight on Tom's part.

No matter. They were here and she longed to know what they contained. Tiffany twirled the satin ribbon on the largest box around her finger before peeling the envelope off the top of the package. She ran a fingertip under the seal and pulled out the card:

Pack your bags. To celebrate our second Anniversary together, I have a special trip planned. I know you've always wanted to travel to Italy, and we have three whole weeks before we have to be back in school. Firenze, Roma, and Venezia are all on the agenda.

Merry Christmas and Happy Anniversary.

All my love, Aiden

A tear trickled down her cheek and splashed onto the festive wrapping, leaving a salty stain. She opened the enclosed paper, the words blurring as she scanned the itinerary for the trip they'd never take. He'd been apologetic that his exams had prevented them from doing much for their second anniversary, but this gift took her breath away. They were to have left last week after he'd written his final exam.

All my love. Fresh tears trickled down her cheeks. Instead of embarking on an exciting holiday with her husband, she'd spent the time pacing and wrestling with regrets.

Tiffany summoned the courage to tug open the ribbon of the next box. It contained an ornate silver frame displaying two of her favorite pictures of her and Aiden. She traced a fingertip over each letter of the fine engraving that commemorated their second anniversary.

Next she opened a velvet box. The glittering diamond and platinum heart-shaped pendant nested inside was one she'd admired on an afternoon shopping trip. With a sad smile, she looped it around her neck and fastened the chain, lifting her trembling hand to her chest. Another sweet and thoughtful gift that made her want to weep.

Finally, she unwrapped the expensive set of art pencils she'd been pining for ever since classes had started in the fall.

Each and every gift made her heartache double. If she weren't so incredibly stupid, she'd be sitting in a trattoria in Rome sipping fine Italian wine with her husband. Instead, she sat here contemplating all the might-have-beens. Every former friend in their group would hate her forever. Like she hated herself.

As she curled up on the bed, she closed her eyes and let the teardrops fall.

Chapter 19

Aiden

Tom poked his head in the door of Aiden's bedroom. "Hey, get your ass in gear."

"I'll be there in a minute." Aiden pulled on his fleece and wandered into the kitchen, double-checking his pack and shoving the water bottle and proffered thermos of hot coffee inside. "Thanks." He tilted his head as the familiar thumping of rotor blades reached his ears.

"No problem." Tom waved him toward the door. "Let's go. Our ride's here."

Aiden stepped out, his smile widening as the helicopter touched down, confirming their destination on this bright and sunny, but crisp December morning. He checked his gear one last time before they loaded their equipment into the carrier and hopped into the back. Leaning back, he glanced at Tom who also sported a huge grin.

Aiden admired the vista of sparkling white powder that opened up below them as they rose into the air. Once they were at the top, they wasted no time strapping on their skis.

Tom had opted not to travel to Chicago for Christmas. Instead, he'd coaxed Aiden onto an airplane bound for Colorado. His friend had scored them a luxurious ski chalet and had booked it until after New Year's.

This alternative suited Aiden perfectly. When everything had blown apart, he'd revised his holiday plans from romantic trip to Italy to lazing around in bed and drinking excessively. Tom, however, refused to let him spend the holidays alone. His best friend had dropped everything to help Aiden lease a new apartment, buy furniture, pack his belongings, and move them to his new home.

After a thumbs up at his best friend, Aiden adjusted his goggles and soon they were both flying down the slope. Skiing was second nature, as they'd both spent many winter days on the hill in various countries and locations.

By mid-afternoon, when they did their last run, Aiden was experiencing an odd sense of exhilaration. The fresh mountain air and a day on the slopes was just what he needed to forget his troubles. At least for a little while.

At seven on New Year's Eve, they arrived at the restaurant where Tom had booked reservations. They were seated near the fireplace which crackled merrily and cast a pleasant glow over the room.

They chatted idly about the day on the slopes over their meals, and then ordered coffee.

"Tom?" Aiden fiddled with his spoon. "Thank you."

"For what?"

"For saving my ass. I've been less than cooperative, but I wanted you to know I appreciate everything you've done. I don't know where I'd be if you hadn't tracked me down and hauled me out of that hotel room."

"You'd do it for me."

"Sure, but you're always too together for me to ever repay the favor. Yet you've done it for me more than once. I wish I'd listened to you and Ryan. It was stupid to marry her, and now …"

"You've done a lot for me, and you're virtually my brother. I'll always be there." Tom sighed. "I wish we'd been wrong. It all seemed to be going so well."

"Yeah, I thought so too. But what do I know? Nothing, apparently." Aiden stared into his cup. "Did you know I'd planned to surprise her with a three-week tour of romantic Italian cities? Like a complete idiot, I felt bad that we couldn't celebrate our anniversary because of my final exam. I don't even know how long her affair was going on, but the only one who ended up surprised was me. I trusted her."

"I'm sorry. I can't even imagine what you're going through right now."

"And you gave up your family holiday to babysit me. I'm sorry you missed it."

"I'm not. Truly, Aiden, I don't mind. This has been an awesome trip, and it's not over yet. Two single guys, several feet of fresh powder, and if I'm not mistaken, two lovely ladies who have been making eyes at us all through dinner. Given the circumstances, you even get to call dibs."

Aiden rolled his eyes. "I already did the whole payback thing in New York."

"This isn't payback, man. Do you see any hope of reviving your marriage?"

"Nope. I'm done."

"Then don't sweat it. Have some fun. Decide quick, they're coming this way. In or out?"

Aiden peered out of the corner of his eye, appraising the two women who were definitely taking an interest in them. "In."

The first day back after New Year's was a struggle for Aiden, but he pried himself out of bed, showered, and dressed. *Fake it till you make it.* That had become his new motto. As if pretending his life could be fixed would make everything better.

The knock on his door had him emitting a long sigh, but he peeked through the viewer into the hallway before opening the door. "Hey, Matthias. How's it going?" He stepped back, allowing his friend to step inside the apartment.

His friend allowed a non-committal shrug, the corners of his lips tugging downward. Upon closer inspection, the dark circles and scruffy beginnings of a beard were evident, as were the red-rimmed eyes.

"Dude. You look worse than I feel," Aiden said.

Matthias scoffed. "Christmas sucked for both of us." The man shoved his hands into his pockets. "I found out that *it's not you it's me* actually means *I'm already fucking some other guy*."

"Damn." Aiden puffed out a stream of air. "Sadly, I get how you feel. You heard?"

"The basics. You left your wife?" His friend glanced around. "Not quite as fancy as the other place, but it's cozy."

"It is that."

The new apartment was on the other side of the campus, about as far away from Tiffany as he could manage. Though tiny, it was clean and close enough to walk to the university, so he was satisfied for now.

"How are you holding up?" Aiden slung his backpack over one shoulder.

"I'll survive. Did you want to stop for a coffee on the way in?"

"Sure." He locked the door and loped down the stairs after Matthias, and they fell into step as they headed toward the small coffee shop down the block.

"I'm really sorry, Aiden," Matthias said after half a block. "Here I am, feeling all sorry for myself but at least Tess broke up with me before she moved on. I don't know how you restrained yourself from killing the bastard. What does Tiffany have to say?"

"I don't know who he is." Aiden scrubbed a hand through his hair and pictured the mess of blood gushing over the man's features. Given the distinct crunching sound, he was sure he had broken the guy's nose, but that was about all he remembered until he found himself on the side of I-95 puking his guts out. Everything else seemed hazy. "I haven't seen her since the day I found them. Nothing she has to say interests me in the least."

"That's it?" The guy shuffled his feet along the cement. "Maybe I'm an idiot, but I would do pretty much anything to get Tess back. I always thought we'd get married and have kids. When I left, she promised she'd wait for me."

"There's no such thing as happily-ever-after." Aiden snorted. "I'll never allow another woman to reel me in with her bullshit promises. It's ridiculous to believe in forever."

"Yeah, I suppose you're right." Matthias held the door open and motioned for Aiden to enter the shop. "Maybe that's the lesson here. Women can never be trusted, even when they swear they love you."

⌒

Three weeks later, Aiden stepped out of the lecture hall and turned to Will and Matthias. "Should we order pizza?" he asked. They were about to start a major study session at Will's apartment. The final months of classes were speeding by, and Aiden embraced the distraction. Keeping his mind focused on anything besides the collapse of his marriage

"Don't look now, but you have company." Will nudged him in the ribs.

Aiden looked up, narrowing his eyes as he spotted the blonde woman standing only a few feet away.

She shuffled her feet and peered at him, twisting and tugging her hair like she might yank a chunk of it out of her scalp.

The worst part was, Aiden wasn't sure she knew that she radiated this mea culpa guilt-inducing little-girl-lost vibe when something was truly wrong. The pang ran straight to his gut. *How did we get here, to this place?*

"You okay?" Will threw a glance his way. "Want us to stick around?"

"No, I've got it. I'll meet you at your place. I can't avoid her forever." *As much as I want to.* Aiden slung his bag over his shoulder as he approached her.

"Hi." She bit her lip and yanked at the lock of hair wrapped around her finger.

"What do you want?" He crossed his arms as he halted several steps away.

Her red-rimmed puffy eyes blinked and she bowed her head. "Can we talk? Maybe over there?" She motioned to a quiet corner out of the flow of students hurrying past on their way to class.

"There's nothing to say." Aiden shoved his hands into his pockets and dragged in a breath. He fought the urge to tuck back the wisp of hair that had fallen across her face.

"Please?" She tugged at her hair even harder. "It's important."

"Five minutes. That's it." Aiden followed her.

"First of all, I'm sorry." She turned toward him. "It just … happened."

"Your clothes just happened to drop off your body, and you just happened to have sex with some guy in our bed?" He paused for a moment, but she remained silent. "Whatever. I'm over it and we're done. Anything else?"

She sucked in a long, audible stream of air. "I'm pregnant."

Aiden's breath caught in his chest. "You're fucking kidding, right?"

"No." Head still bowed, she wagged it back and forth while avoiding his gaze. "I went to the doctor, and I'm definitely pregnant."

"Fuck." Aiden rubbed a hand through his hair and fought the sick feeling curling through him. "Is it mine? Or his?"

Tiffany stared at her feet, still twisting the hair around her finger and tugging at it.

"Damn it, Tiffany." Aiden sank onto a bench and dropped his head into his hand. *Just when I thought it couldn't get any worse ...* "You don't even know, do you?"

"I'm sorry." She sat beside him, clenching her hands in her lap. The diamond ring on her left hand glittered and winked at him. "I'm about seven weeks along."

"That's fucking awesome news. Thanks. That's exactly what I needed to hear about now." Aiden's stomach turned. "So now what? Did you tell what's-his-face yet?"

"Derrick," she whispered and shook her head. "I thought I should talk to you first. I'm having the baby and I think the baby is yours."

"And how would you know that?" *Derrick.* He cringed. That day he'd been so destroyed, he hadn't even recognized who had been on top of his wife. Afterward, he'd avoided thinking about it. Now it made total sense. "How long were you screwing him? All those late nights at work?"

"It only happened once."

"Did you use condoms?"

She shook her head.

"Shit." His eyes burned and his chest constricted.

"I'm sorry. It happened so fast. I promise it was only once, and I regret it more than I can say."

Only? He fought down his building anger. Once was enough to end their marriage and that she could say it had *only* been the one time was almost more than he could bear. Cheating was cheating. "Happy fucking anniversary to us, right?"

She looked away before she pulled a crumpled paper from her bag. "The doctor gave me this with the dates on it."

Aiden accepted and scanned it, the words blurring as reality set in. "You can't possibly know whose kid it is. For you to say it's mine is bullshit and you know it. Based on these dates, it's probably his." He shoved it back at her. "Good luck. You should see what *Derrick* has to say. I'm out."

He rose from the bench and forced himself to walk away. The moment he'd rounded the corner, he leaned against the wall, tipping back his head and closing his eyes. Something that should have been wonderful news simply burned. He didn't feel even the tiniest flicker of excitement or joy. What were the odds that the baby was his? Physically possible, but highly unlikely.

With shaking hands, he dialed his phone. "Tom."

"Aiden? Are you okay?"

"No." Thoughts spun through his mind as he pressed his back against the wall, curling up his knees as he slid downward into a heap.

"What's happening?" The background noise around Tom became muted. "Talk to me."

"She's pregnant." The words left his mouth, nothing but a faint and fuzzy buzz.

"Wait … Who?" Tom's sharp inhale was audible. "Tiffany?"

"She has no clue who's it is."

"Damn."

"What do I do?"

"What can you do? There's no way of knowing until the baby is born."

"How do I get through months of not knowing? This kid could just as easily be his as mine. I'm freaking out. I wanted to put it all behind me, and now that's impossible." He dropped his chin to his chest, fighting back the tears gathering behind his eyes. His life was falling apart over this woman for the second time. It felt like fate playing a cruel joke.

"There's no easy answer. Until you perform a DNA test, you won't know."

"In the meantime, there will be doctor's appointments, and ultrasounds, and all of that. So, I don't go to any of it and later find out I missed out on being there for my kid. Or I go to all of it and then, in the end, find out I'm not the father. I'm so screwed."

"I'm on my way."

"You have classes."

"You need me. You hang in there and we'll talk it through. Don't do anything stupid in the meantime. Promise?"

"Yeah." Aiden's head bobbed in agreement though he wasn't sure what Tom imagined he'd do. He couldn't even make his limbs respond to stand.

"Go home and wait for me. No drinking or bars." Tom's voice sounded hollow and echoed as the background sound of a metal door clanging carried through the phone. "I'm getting in my car right now. I'll be there soon, and we'll sort it out."

After they'd hung up, Aiden wrapped his arms around his knees and closed his eyes. His life kept getting worse and nothing would ever be the same.

Chapter 20

Tiffany

After a sleepless night, Tiffany shuffled along the street rubbing at her tear-stained cheeks. In the past, Aiden had forgiven her stupid mistakes, but this time she feared there was no way back. This was far beyond a simple error, and now there was a baby involved. She hoped the child was Aiden's, as she longed to build a family with him, but she dreaded that wasn't the case.

And she had to face the reality that she might be alone when this baby arrived. The thought filled her with dread. Maybe if she gave Aiden some time and space, he'd come around. Dropping the bomb on him the way she had may have been unfair.

She glanced at her watch. Derrick had agreed to meet her for coffee so she should head to the café. Ever since that day when Aiden had broken the man's nose, Tiffany had kept her distance, allowing him to avoid her without protest.

"Hey." She slid into the seat opposite him, cringing at the faint yellowish tinge that spread across his cheekbone.

He eyed her warily. "Hey, yourself."

"I'm sorry about your face," she said.

"So you've said about a hundred times. I didn't know your husband packed such a punch. He doesn't look that big."

"He works out. You should see him with his shirt off." Tiffany twirled a strand of hair as the waitress came by to take her order. "Peppermint tea, please?"

"Yeah, no thanks. I hope I never see him again." Derrick sipped his coffee. "Herbal tea? You're usually a caffeine hound."

She smiled faintly at the waitress as she set the small pot and a fresh teacup in front of her. "How have you been?" Tiffany dunked the teabag, twining the string around her finger.

"Now that my face is healing? Better, I suppose. I've thought about pressing charges. I still might."

Tiffany lifted her gaze to his. "Against Aiden?" She shook her head. "No, you can't."

"He broke my nose."

Tiffany rubbed at her temple. "Because we were having sex in our bed, you idiot. He was upset, he's not like that usually," she whispered, glancing at the surrounding tables.

"So what? I have medical bills I can't pay."

"Don't, Derrick. It's a bad idea."

"Why? You're protecting him after what he did?"

"Trust me, you do not want to take a run at Aiden. He'll mop the floor with you. Do you know who his father is? Or his grandfather?"

Derrick raised a brow. "Like I should be scared?"

"Yes, you should. His dad is an Assistant DA in New York City. His grandfather is a partner in one of the biggest criminal law firms in Chicago. Two of his best friends are studying law. There's no way you'd win. Trust me, you don't want to be on the wrong side of the Hamilton family." She picked at the corner of the wrapper from her teabag. "Just drop it."

"So he's all connected and he gets away with messing up my face?"

"It was my fault, Derrick. What we did was wrong." Tiffany sniffled, unable to look at him. "If you want to blame someone, blame me. Aiden could have done a lot more damage to you than he did. You're lucky he walked away."

"Lucky?" Derrick sat back. "A broken nose is lucky?"

"He didn't beat the crap out of you, so yeah, it is."

"What did he do to you?"

"He left me. That's my punishment. I destroyed my marriage." *And for what?* "I have something to tell you."

"Now what?"

She closed her eyes. "I'm pregnant."

"What? No way."

Tears flooded her eyes. "Based on the timing, the baby might be yours. We didn't use a condom, remember?"

"Or it's his?" He glowered. "You had sex with him? After us?"

"Not after." She hadn't even seen Aiden until she tracked him down to announce her pregnancy. "A few days before." She motioned between them.

"He's my husband." Or, he was her husband. Now she wasn't sure. She pressed a finger against her ring, the exquisite diamond digging into her flesh. One day, she'd have to remove it, but right now, she carried a faint hope that her husband might forgive her. "You and Annalise always made snide comments about our fights and the make-up sessions, so don't pretend you didn't know."

"You're disgusting. Now you're knocked up and sniffing around like I'll support you and the brat that's not even mine?" Derrick scoffed. "You picked the wrong guy. I'm a broke art student. Why don't you hit up your rich husband?"

Tiffany clenched her hands around her cup. She couldn't tell Derrick that she didn't want him or his support. The child would have to come first, no matter her feelings on the situation. Even if it was Aiden she wanted, not Derrick. It had never been Derrick.

"Oh, right. He dumped you and you're looking for a convenient target to support you." He snatched his coat from the back of his chair. "Lose my number, you stupid slut."

The door fell shut behind him as he stormed from the restaurant, leaving her with her head bowed over the rapidly cooling tea. The words stung, but his departure left her relieved. If he chose to walk away, it equaled one less complication.

―≼

The next day started off rough. Tiffany spent several minutes poised over the porcelain toilet bowl in the master bath, heaving until her stomach had emptied. She followed that performance with a hot shower and dressed in baggy sweatpants before forcing down a slice of toast and a cup of peppermint tea, hoping she'd make it through class without embarrassing herself.

The short trek to school refreshed her somewhat, but even the best skill with the makeup brush couldn't hide the dark circles under her eyes or the puffy redness. She slumped into a seat, taking care to sit several tables away from Derrick who curled his lip and looked away.

"You look like crap." Annalise's lip curled as she hovered over Tiffany. "I heard your husband left you. Serves you right. That's what happens when you get greedy." She tossed her hair over her shoulder and stalked to the table in the far corner away from both Tiffany and Derrick.

More people entered the room and claimed tables, but the ones closest to her were the last to be filled. Tiffany hunched her shoulders and kept her head down, trying to ignore the whispers and looks coming her way. By the end of the class, she could scarcely hold back the tears. He'd told everyone. What or how much, she wasn't sure, but it was enough to send her scurrying through the exit doors at the end of the first period.

She trudged home, entering the silent apartment and dropping her bag by the front door, kicking off her shoes and leaving them where they landed. Aiden would hate it, but she supposed it didn't much matter. He was gone.

―

The next morning when her alarm rang, she smacked it and rolled over, sucking in breaths to settle the nausea. She closed her eyes and returned to the solace of sleep, waking only when the light had dimmed in the late afternoon. Her stomach rumbled so she dragged herself from bed and down to the kitchen, digging in the fridge for some leftovers. Then she snuggled on the couch under her favorite blanket, watching mindless sitcoms until the early hours of the morning before crawling into her bed again.

This became her routine. Drag herself from bed in the late morning or early afternoon, splash icy water on her face, and then retreat to the sofa to binge on television and the occasional order of greasy takeout. Anything resembling fresh food had long since been emptied from the fridge, and it seemed she no longer had a housekeeper to take care of the shopping and cleaning even though she'd been allowed to keep the apartment.

She didn't much care. Without Aiden, nothing mattered. For the first two days, she dialed his number every few hours and listened to his voice mail, but after a few messages, she stopped begging him to call her back. That last look he'd given her as he'd said *I'm out* and walked away was forever etched in her memory.

Visiting him was as pointless as bothering to bridge the gap with Derrick. Two men and neither of them wanted her. They viewed her as a worthless piece of trash carrying an unwanted child.

Today was no different. She dropped onto the couch, dragged the blanket over herself, and closed her eyes as the television droned in the background.

"Fuck. This place is a disaster."

The voice made her jump. "Aiden?" She sat, scooping her stringy hair back from her face. "What are you doing here? How did you get in?"

He held up his key. "One of your professors called and said you'd dropped off the map."

"Why'd they call you?" With the blanket tucked under her chin, she curled into a ball, combing her fingers through her tangled curls.

"I'm your emergency contact." He stood in the middle of the room and surveyed the apartment. "You want to attract a pack of rats?" His lip curled as he lifted the week-old takeout container off the coffee table with two fingers and tossed it aside. He swept off a corner and sat. "You look like hell. Have you been eating?"

She shrugged.

"Have you been to see your doctor? Or taken any vitamins?" His brows rose as he wrinkled his nose. "Or practiced any sort of personal hygiene in the past two weeks?"

"What do you care?"

"I'm not thrilled with this situation." He scrubbed a hand over his jaw. "However, that baby could be mine. This whole thing …" As he shook his head, he leveled his gaze at her. "You're pregnant. The baby is an innocent party in this whole stinking mess. Take care of yourself, for fuck's sake. At least do it for the kid. Get your ass off that couch and take a damn shower."

She had no choice. The obstinate jerk would make sure she did what he said. Wrapping the blanket around her, she shuffled toward the stairs, clomping slowly upward and then down the hall to the bathroom. The water hissed through the shower head as she cranked it on full blast and held a hand under the spray until it warmed up enough for her to step into the stall.

"Use lots of shampoo on that rat's nest."

"What are you doing in here?" She covered herself with her hands.

"Like I haven't already seen it." He scoffed. "Gross. This blanket should be torched," he muttered before yanking the door closed behind him.

By the time she dragged herself out of the bathroom wrapped in a towel, the apartment seemed a different place. The washing machine thumped away, the bed had been stripped, and the blinds were all open with a window cracked open to let in a stream of fresh, crisp air.

"Aiden?" She peered over the railing as the apartment door clicked shut. Great. He'd left? "Are you there?"

"I took out the garbage." He crossed his arms. "When did you last eat?"

She shrugged. "I'm not hungry."

"Too bad. Put on some clothes, and we'll buy groceries. The fridge is empty aside from a couple of rotten apples and a carton of sour milk." He waved at her. "Go."

Tiffany picked at the plate of food before her, peeking across the table at Aiden.

After forcing her to the grocery store and stocking her fridge, he'd suggested they visit the small café a few doors down. He hadn't ordered anything aside from a coffee, but he'd made her choose a meal. Now it seemed he was monitoring every bite.

"I screwed up, and now you hate me."

His face remained a blank mask, but his grip tightened on his cup.

"Is there any way you'll forgive me?"

"Why didn't you tell me you were so unhappy?"

"I wasn't unhappy."

"Don't lie." His jaw clenched. "Why else would you do that to me? To us?"

"I don't know why," she whispered. "It just happened."

Aiden hunched his shoulders. "I planned this big trip for us. I figured you deserved it for being so understanding about all the late nights. It turns out I'm a stupid moron. All that time you were …" He rubbed the back of his neck.

"I would have loved it. I'm so sorry."

"Whatever. It's done and there's no going back."

"I love you."

"I wish I believed that." The brief shake of his head and resigned and defeated way he closed his eyes and tipped his head down made her heart ache.

Tiffany longed to wrap her arms around him. To beg for forgiveness. To find a way to ease the pain and disappointment reflected in his eyes when he looked at her. "Whether you believe me or not, it's true."

Aiden's phone buzzed on the table.

Her breath caught as the name appeared across the screen. *Angelica.* "Who's that?"

Aiden flipped his phone face down. "That's none of your business." He rested his left hand on the back, tapping the phone with a finger as it vibrated again.

"Where's your wedding band?" Tiffany's gaze rested on his bare ring finger.

"It's gone on a permanent basis. Our marriage is over. You ended it the moment you decided it was a good idea to fuck Derrick in our bed."

"Who's Angelica."

"Someone I'm seeing." He narrowed his eyes. "It just kind of … happened."

Tears sprang to her eyes. "What? You fell into her bed by complete accident? You made such a big deal about me saying it happened, yet you use that excuse?"

"Huh. Imagine you being upset by that." His mouth set into a grim line. "Now you get how ridiculous you sounded. It didn't just happen. After you chose to break our marriage vows, I chose to have sex with other women. And don't you dare judge me."

"When did it start?" she whispered, nausea rising at the thought of Aiden with another woman. *Women.* Had he said women? "So you've been with more than—" She snapped her mouth closed as his brows rose and a steely glint appeared in his eyes. *Did I really want him to answer that?* "What about the baby?"

A dark look crossed his features. "What about the baby?"

"When I have an ultrasound, I want you to come."

"An ultrasound for the kid that probably isn't mine." He thumped a fist on the table. "Fantastic. I can't wait. Is that other guy planning to join us? Make it a real special occasion?"

Tiffany shook her head and brushed at the tears trickling down her face. "He's out of the picture. Neither of you want me, and neither of you give a crap about this baby. I'm going home." She stumbled to her feet and struggled into her jacket.

"You do that." He pulled out his wallet and dropped some cash on the table. "Get it together. Make sure you book a doctor's appointment."

Anger raged through her. "You're awfully bossy. This kid isn't even yours, remember?" The moment the words left her mouth, she wished she could rewind and take them back. "Aiden," she whispered, reaching toward him.

He gave his head a small shake, directing a scathing look her way as he dodged her outstretched hand. Without a backward glance, he was gone, the door swinging closed behind him.

She brushed at her eyes, pushing down the rage flooding her. She'd made a mistake, but she hadn't seen or been with anyone since that fateful day.

Aiden on the other hand … had he meant for her to see his phone? To drive her insane? He'd outright admitted he'd been with another woman—multiple other women—since he'd walked out the door. Being a man, he could get away with it. If she did it, everyone would call her a slut. She suspected everyone already was as Derrick hadn't been discreet about their involvement.

Derrick's words flashed through her mind. 'No wonder he dumped you. You're disgusting.' Those words taunted her daily. What she'd done to Aiden was repugnant.

Maybe she shouldn't even have this baby. She'd be a terrible mother, and everyone believed her to be a horrible person. Aiden had only come to the apartment day because of the slim chance this baby was his. Everyone else had bought into Derrick's stories and lies.

And eventually, she'd be forced to face the friends who were also Aiden's friends. What he'd told them, she hadn't gathered the courage to ask. Maybe she didn't want to know because having everyone hate her was more than she could take.

Even worse, she had to deal with the issue of whether to tell her parents. Her stomach lurched as the ache grew inside. Another major disappointment that would be even worse if the DNA testing revealed that Aiden wasn't the baby's father.

Chapter 21

Aiden

Aiden nursed his third drink, keeping his head down as he struggled with the overwhelming emotions. Had she meant it? Or was it retaliation?

Maybe he shouldn't have baited her with Angelica, but the call had come at that opportune moment. His wife acted like they could save their relationship. Like she believed there was something left to be salvaged.

The inevitable chorus of *I told you so* from his family and friends would be unbearable. That, on top of her taunt about the kid's parentage seemed unusually cruel and showed him her unsavory and vindictive side. *Why did I ever love her?*

He tipped back his glass, draining the last of the amber liquid before motioning at the bartender to hit him with another. The moment it was poured, he tossed it back, tapping on the side of his glass for an immediate refill. Now he'd numbed the pain, even if only a little, he could call his best friend. "Am I a complete idiot?" he asked.

"How much have you had to drink?" Tom's voice was laced with concern.

"One or two," he mumbled.

"Or five or six." Tom sighed. "What happened?"

"Apparently, the kid's not mine."

"Shit."

"It might be her getting back at me. Or she's putting me in my rightful place."

"And where's that?"

Aiden lifted a shoulder and scoffed. *Damned if I know.*

"So?" Tom asked

"Angelica called."

"Angelica?" he asked. "You've been in contact?"

"You could say that." He pictured the last two weekends he'd spent in New York with the beautiful, though slightly older woman. His classes were suffering, but right now he didn't much care. Soothing the pain seemed more important.

"What does Angelica have to do with Tiffany?"

"Tiff saw the call display." Aiden gulped down his drink in two swallows. "Whatever. It changes nothing. The first appointment will be soon. Should I go?"

"If you don't, you'll never forgive yourself."

"Have you ever heard a baby's heartbeat?"

"Not in real life."

Aiden massaged his temples, trying to sort his jumbled thoughts. Everything grew fuzzy and grayish.

"Are you there?" Tom asked.

"What if I can't walk away?"

"You need to take that chance." His friend emitted another long sigh. "This isn't a situation you'll get through without scars. Even if the baby isn't yours…"

After a silent moment, Aiden asked, "What?"

"Is that other guy planning to step up at any point?"

"He walked." He scoffed. "It was only once. It didn't mean anything."

"It meant something to you."

Aiden closed his eyes, wishing he could block out the horrible images. He could still see them. Hear them. Maybe now she was getting a taste of how it felt.

"Damn woman," Tom said under his breath. "I wish I was there."

What could he say after her epic betrayal of trust? The complete destruction of a relationship he'd held close even over thousands of miles and three years of endless time? He hauled in a shaky breath.

"Damn," his friend muttered. "Here's the legal situation. You're the presumptive parent of this child as you're married to her. You admit there's a chance it's yours, which is the best case scenario. At the very least, she'll get child support out of you. Even if DNA testing proves you're not the father, it could be a tough fight. The courts strive to give children the benefit of two parents."

"I can't take her back."

"I'd never even suggest it, but the kid needs a father. As much as I hate this situation, this child needs you. Imagine their life without a father."

Aiden huffed out a breath. "Get to the point."

"Two words."

"Which are?"

"David Baxter."

He groaned. "You had to go there."

"Sorry, but Tiffany's home life was crap. We all know it. If you walk away and refuse to support them, even for a short time while you sort this out, she'll end up at home and under her daddy's thumb. She won't have much choice and that kid will suffer."

"So pretend?" Aiden rubbed a hand through his hair.

"Go to the appointments. You have no choice."

Aiden signaled the bartender for another drink. "I'll take it under advisement, counselor."

"If that's unpalatable, there's another option."

"What's that?"

"Adoption."

Aiden sucked in a breath as the nausea rose.

"It's worth considering. There's a waiting list for babies in every state."

"No," Aiden said in a low voice. "A hard no. If the kid's mine, I can't. If the kid isn't mine, I have no right to even suggest it."

"Maybe I should get in the car? You're in rough shape."

"I'll manage. You can't drive here every time I have a crisis. If you did that, you'd never graduate." Aiden rubbed his temple.

"You'll get through this."

"I sure hope so." He tapped the rim of his glass, thankful when the bartender poured another.

"I'm here if you need to talk. If it becomes too much, get on a plane and come stay with me for a bit."

"I don't know how to do this. I thought we were forever." He clenched his lids against the burn behind his eyes and pinched the bridge of his nose.

Once he'd hung up, he hit his speed dial, grateful when he got her voice mail. "It's me," he said. "Phone me when you have the first appointment booked with your doctor. Even though you hate me, it's no longer about us." He stabbed at the button to disconnect the call and waved over his glass to order another round.

He didn't hear from Tiffany for three days, but finally, he received a text.

Thursday. One p.m.

An address for the doctor's office popped up on his screen. Aiden tucked his phone into his pocket and picked up the cue.

Will appeared with two drinks and offered one to Aiden. "The lovely Angelica sending love messages?"

"Tiffany has a doctor's appointment."

"You're going through with it?" Will lined up a shot, breaking with a clatter of balls.

"Do I have a choice? Whether or not the kid is mine, the kid will be mine." Aiden drained his glass as Will took another shot.

"Hardly seems fair. She cheats, and you get stuck with the kid." Will shook his head.

"Welcome to the wonderful world of being screwed over by a woman. Word of advice. If you ever think about marriage, don't." He waved his empty glass at the waitress and lined up his first shot. "Run as far and as fast as you can." The ball skittered across the table as he slammed it with the cue, sinking the two solids in its path.

"Easy man," Will said as he stepped out of the line of fire.

Aiden accepted his drink from the waitress and downed it, setting the empty glass on the tray before she had a chance to walk away. "Another would be great. Better make it a double." He turned to contemplate his next move.

"You know those are meant to be sipped, right?"

Aiden squinted at Will before proceeding to sink two more shots. When he missed the next one, he motioned to the table. "All yours."

"What does everyone else say?" Will chalked his cue.

"Everyone as in Tom?" Aiden accepted his fresh drink from the waitress. "We haven't shared the news. It's not exactly cause for joyful celebration." He leaned a hip against the table. "Neither of us are close with our families." Aiden shrugged.

"Did you two talk about kids before you got married?"

A pang of regret hit him. No matter how hard he'd tried over the past two years, she'd refused to discuss their past. "I love kids and I want a family, but not like this. This baby might be mine, but …" He lay his pool cue on the table and placed his flattened palms on the edge. How could he express the turmoil in his soul? The guilt, the fear, and the overwhelming sense of hopelessness that tore him apart inside?

Will patted his shoulder. "You've had enough to drink. Let's get you home."

⁓

Tiffany looked up from where she sat on the edge of her chair. "I didn't think you'd come."

"Neither did I."

She clenched her hands in her lap and slid back in her seat, eyeing the chair next to her.

Aiden sat and hunched forward to rest his arms on his knees, keeping his head bowed. "I won't take it out on the kid. I need to be here."

An uneasy silence fell over them, and Tiffany fidgeted in her seat, twining a finger into her hair and tugging at the lock.

"Stop it." Aiden untangled her fingers, freezing for a moment before he yanked his hand away.

Tiffany clutched the hem of her sweater and looked away, giving an audible sniffle.

Aiden clenched his jaw, biting back the words that wanted to escape.

"Why are you so mean?" she whispered. "It's not like you look so damn great, showing up hung-over."

He closed his eyes and turned his head away. How could she berate him after what she'd done?

"Tiffany Hamilton?" The nurse beckoned from across the room.

"You can leave." Tiffany averted her gaze as she rose from her seat. "I don't need you."

Aiden narrowed his eyes but followed as the nurse led them down the hallway and motioned for him to go into an exam room.

"We'll weigh you and then you can change into a gown."

He paced the tiny room, stopping to inspect the chart on the wall showing the stages of growth each week. Ten weeks and the baby would be around an inch long.

Tiffany entered the room behind him. "You're still here."

He shrugged and focused on the floor as she peeled off her sweater and changed into the gown.

"Why so shy? It's not like you haven't seen me naked."

"Things have changed."

"Fine. I'm decent." Tiffany perched on the exam table, rubbing her arms. "It's cold in here." She tilted her head. "Are you planning on being in the room when the baby is born?"

The doctor tapped on the door and slipped into the room. "Good morning, Tiffany. I see we have a scan scheduled today." She smiled at Aiden. "You must be the husband."

He nodded.

The doctor asked several questions and performed the pre-natal exam, and then moved the ultrasound machine beside the bed. "Let's listen."

The whoosh of the baby's heartbeat filled the room.

Aiden dug his nails into his palm, avoiding looking at Tiffany as the image appeared on the screen. He scrubbed a hand over his rough stubble, swallowing hard to dislodge the lump in his throat. Seeing the tiny form made this all real. Suddenly, he was transported to another time and place.

"I'll print pictures and a video if you like," the doctor said.

He answered Tiffany's furtive glance with a lift of one shoulder.

"That would be great." Tiffany's smile didn't quite reach her eyes.

"The baby looks good, but I'm concerned about your weight. You're too thin." The doctor made a few notes and looked up from the chart. "Are you eating properly?"

Tiffany bit her lip but nodded. "I've had a lot of morning sickness but I'm trying."

"More protein, lots of fluids, avoid stress, and take your vitamins. By the next visit, I'd like you to have gained several pounds. Any questions?"

Aiden shook his head and stared at the floor.

The doctor gave them a quizzical look before she cleared her throat. "I'll see you in two weeks. You can make another appointment on the way out." She pulled the door closed as she left.

"This is how it's going to be?" Tiffany slid from the table. "I'll be doing this alone?"

"I'm sorry if I can't be, or do whatever it is you think I should. Do you have any idea how hard this is? To be in this room with my *wife* and not know? Maybe you've come to terms with it, but you're certain this kid is yours." He reached for the door handle. "Excuse me for not jumping on board with the *enthusiasm* you seem to expect of me."

She placed a hand on his arm. "I can't do this by myself."

"Oh, don't worry, honey." He leveled his icy gaze at her as he brushed away her fingers. "You have me. You can keep the apartment. I'll pay the bills and come to every single appointment. I'll even be there when the baby is born and be the kid's dad. But stop with those looks. Don't you get what you've done?" He yanked the door open, unable to stand another second of her charade.

The woman seemed oblivious to the fact she'd broken him, leaving nothing but a vacant space that had formerly been filled with amazing hopes and dreams. He'd never love another woman, ever again. The price was far too high.

Chapter 22

Tiffany

The days had crept by since Aiden had stormed out of the exam room, and she'd heard nothing from him.

He had kept his word though. Erika had reappeared over the weekend to give the apartment a thorough cleaning and stock the fridge full of healthy eating options. The woman had even provided two days worth of meals, trying to tempt her to eat more.

She did her best even though most mornings she felt horrible and had little appetite. The worst part was dealing with Aiden's absence and the reality that this time, forgiveness would be nearly impossible to earn. The love she'd always seen reflected in his eyes had disappeared, leaving a glazed-bordering-on-blank expression that seemed to morph into hatred at a moment's notice.

The only thing that kept her going was the faint hope that the baby would bring them back together. The promise he'd made to be a proper father to this child hadn't escaped her. As grudging as the gesture seemed, it meant he'd be in her life. Over time, she might have a chance at redemption.

When she arrived at the doctor's office for her next appointment, Aiden was already there. She contemplated him, noting the dark circles under his eyes and the scruffy appearance of his face. Not that she minded the rough sexy stubble, but it pained her to see him so devastated by everything. And it was entirely her fault.

"How are you?" She lowered herself into the chair next to him.

He lifted a shoulder and stared at his folded hands.

"You didn't get this at our last appointment." She offered him the copy of the ultrasound picture she'd tucked into her purse.

"Thanks," he said in a low voice, staring at the image for a moment before he pulled out his wallet and tucked it inside.

She cleared her throat. "Have you told anyone about the baby?"

After a glance her way, he said, "Tom knows, of course. As does Will, Ben, and Matthias. You?"

Tiffany gave her head the tiniest shake. "I'm sorry." She looked his way. "I haven't said that enough, but I'm truly sorry for what happened. I love you, so much."

"Don't." He rubbed a hand over his eyes, his brow furrowing. "It's too late for apologies and platitudes and all of that. Let's just …" His chin tipped down as a saddened expression took over. "You'll hear from my lawyer soon, so you should retain counsel and think about what you want in the divorce."

"I don't want a divorce."

"I'll give you a fair settlement," he said without so much as a twitch to acknowledge he'd heard her comment, "and child support for the baby's needs."

Tiffany clasped her hands in her lap. No point in pushing the stubborn man. It would only force him to keep her at a greater distance. Over the years, she'd grown to know the man far too well. But she couldn't prevent herself from whispering, "I love you. That will never change."

Her heart sank as his lips set into a grim line and he shifted in his seat, turning away from her.

"Tiffany?" The nurse smiled and beckoned from across the room.

She rose, keeping her hands clenched together to avoid reaching for Aiden. Last time she was pregnant … *No*. The thought was immediately banished from her mind. Reliving the memory was far too painful to even contemplate, and discussing it with her husband, who was soon to be her ex-husband if he had his way, was impossible.

To her relief, he followed her across the room and down the short, stark white hallway into an exam room, accepting her bag while she slipped off her shoes and allowed the nurse to lead her to a scale just outside the room.

"Good. You've gained a little weight." The woman jotted down notes on the chart and ushered Tiffany into the room again. "Change into the gown and the doctor will be right in to perform an exam."

Aiden sat in the chair in the corner, staring at the floor as she changed, barely lifting his head.

She caught the brief glance he shot toward her belly. Tiffany bit her lip as she adjusted the mint green cotton and slid onto the edge of the table. If she could gather the courage … After a long deep breath, she left her perch and shuffled across the room, stopping in front of him.

His chin rose as he became aware of her presence, a deep furrow in his brow as he stared at her. "What?" he asked in a low, barely audible voice.

Without a word, she took his hand and pressed it to her belly. This small act she hoped would encourage him and allow him to become more involved in the process. Her greatest fear was the emotional distance he'd forced between them and that it might prevent him from bonding with their child. *Our child.* This unbidden thought stole her breath away. After all of this time, they had a chance for a family together. A chance to regain all that had been stolen from them.

Before she could speak, he pulled away, flexing his hand and wiping it on the leg of his jeans as if he could brush away the unpleasant thoughts racing through his head. Or so she assumed from the dark look in his eyes and the derisive curl of his lip.

She opened her mouth, but the door opened.

"How are you today?" The woman's voice asked from behind her.

"Good." Tiffany forced a smile and turned, moving towards the table and clambering on top, the paper crinkling underneath her.

The doctor performed an exam before rubbing the metal end of the Doppler to warm it before searching Tiffany's belly, a smile gracing her lips as the steady and reassuring whoosh of the baby's heartbeat filled the room.

Tiffany stole a glance at Aiden, seeing the tiniest flicker of wonder before he shuttered his emotions and returned to the stony blankness Tiffany had come to fear. Still, there it was, the flash of interest in the baby she'd hoped for. The man was still her Aiden underneath, and she was willing to wait, to exhibit an uncharacteristic patience while he dealt with his anger. And maybe, if she was lucky, he would someday forgive her. Maybe this baby really would bridge the gap between them.

The days and then the weeks passed with little change in their relationship. Aiden showed up for the appointments and inquired on her health, but that blank, sad expression never seemed to leave him.

After their latest appointment, she said, "We should talk about setting up a room for the baby. Will you come shopping with me?"

Aiden lifted a shoulder, his gaze dropping to the slight rounding of her belly. "It's too soon."

"I'm past the twelve week mark." She twirled a lock of hair around her finger. "When are we going to tell our friends?"

His head dipped and he shoved his hands into his pockets as they walked toward the apartment. "You can tell them whatever you want, whenever you want." His tone seemed flat and uninterested.

She heaved a sigh. "I want to tell them we're having a baby. Do you want everyone to know the entire story?" *I sure don't.*

"It's up to you," he said, barely sparing her a glance. "Are you planning to tell your parents you're pregnant?"

"I'm not sure they'll care, but maybe sometime. How about you? Have you told your grandmother or Joel or Ryan? Or Alex?"

He shook his head. "My family wrote me off a long time ago. I'm not sure what to say to anybody else. Maybe it's the *I told you so* I'm not ready to hear."

A pang hit her chest. Maybe he wasn't wrong in that assessment. It took their friends a significant amount of time to accept their marriage and warm up to the idea. Even if neither Jenna nor Alexis had said it, she knew her friends viewed them as too young to make that magnitude of commitment. At least she and Aiden had tried, but it would be tough to come up with an explanation as to why they lived in separate apartments and why they were divorcing even as they welcomed a baby.

She combed her fingers through her hair as she trudged along. Aiden being here was a miracle. She still didn't understand the decision, even if she was grateful he'd chosen to be involved. As hard as she tried to pretend, the inevitable always caught up to her. This baby might not be his. Once the child was born and he could perform a DNA test, he might walk away, leaving her alone to raise the kid. But what other option did she have? She couldn't go through the same feelings as last time. Losing another child and knowing they were out there somewhere wasn't something she'd survive.

Every day she sent her fervent wished out to the universe to make this child Aiden's. To give him a reason to stay. She stole another look at him. He was so familiar and reassuring, yet he acted like a total stranger. She longed to catch his hand, to have him sling an arm around her and pull her to his side as they walked. To plant a kiss on her lips and rest a hand on her belly. To see him smile again, even one single time.

It took great effort on her part to not say it yet again, so she pressed a hand to her chest, repeating the words in her mind. *I love you. I'm sorry. Please forgive me.*

Aiden cleared his throat, breaking into her thoughts. "I have some major exams to study for. We can decorate a nursery once those are over next week." He rubbed at the back of his neck. "Do you even want to be in Philly? Or would you prefer to move to Chicago? You could go to the Art Institute again. I'll get you a place to live and pay the tuition."

"Are you moving back?" Her heart lifted at the idea. Philly contained nothing but bad memories.

"After I'm finished medical school, I plan to request a residency in Chicago."

"How would that work?" She frowned. "You have another year of school. What about the baby?"

"I'll travel to Chicago on weekends." He shrugged. "You're unhappy here. You should go home and get on with your life."

"Or is it that you want to get on with yours?" She folded her arms across her chest. "It's an easy out for you, right?"

"Easy?" He scoffed. "You haven't been happy for more than a day at a time since we got married. Philly will never be home for you, and I don't want to keep you away from your friends and family."

"So you'd have me to believe this is altruistic and to make me happy? Or is it out of sight, out of mind for a child you don't believe is even yours?"

"What the hell do you want from me?" He halted, a dark look on his face. "I'm trying to make this easier for you so maybe you can see your damn mother and have some help. And maybe, just maybe, you'll get your crap together and finally be happy."

"What about you?"

"Me? I'm buried in classes and exams and I can't provide the support you need. This is the wrong time for all of this, even if this kid is …."

"Yours? You want to dump us. This isn't for me at all."

"I meant what I said, Tiffany. Whether this kid is mine or not, the kid is mine, but you moping around in Philly isn't healthy for either of us. I can't give you the attention you seek and you hate it here, so I'm finding a solution. It's only until I graduate and then I'll move to Chicago."

"I'm not leaving without you." Her head wagged back and forth as she forced away the picture of existing without Aiden. It wouldn't be conducive for them to get back together if they lived in different states.

"It would make it easier to explain."

"What?"

"Our divorce. I'll hold off filing until after the baby is born. You move back to Chicago and tell everyone that you want to be closer to home during your leave from school. I'll set you up in an apartment. In fact"—he reached into his inner pocket and held out a paper—"I found this place. It doesn't look like much, but it's an entire floor and the location is amazing. After it's fixed up, it'll be great."

Tiffany studied the real estate listing. "You're thinking of buying it?"

"I already did. It was undervalued because it needs substantial renovations, but it's a Gold Coast location with a lake view." He shrugged. "The architect is already working on it. Once you're in Chicago, you can live there. You can return to the Art Institute and in a few months, I'll send the papers and we can get it over with."

And there it was. The inevitable end. Aiden firmly pushing her away with both hands. If he made her go, the chances that she'd win him back would decrease every single day they were apart.

When Aiden's phone rang seconds later, and he slipped it from his pocket to peer at the screen, it seemed like too good of an opportunity to pass up. Tiffany craned her neck and caught a glimpse of the screen. *Giannelli, Angelica.* Combined with a New York prefix.

Her husband squinted her way as he silenced the incoming call and tucked the mobile out of the sight of her curious eyes.

"Are you still seeing her?" Tiffany whispered.

"Who?" That award-winning blank expression took over again.

"That woman. Angelica. Are you sleeping with her? Or is it someone else now?"

"It's none of your business." The slight twitch and involuntary touch of his thumb to the bare ring finger of his left hand gave him away. As did the guilt fleeting across his features.

The thought of him in the arms of another woman caused a twinge of jealousy. She struggled with the reality that she pushed him there. If she wanted him back, she'd have to suck it up. "I forgive you," she said softly. "When you're finished punishing me, I'll be waiting."

"Why would I need or even want your forgiveness?" He shook his head. "Don't bother waiting. Plenty of people manage to raise a child without being bound to each other by marriage. I don't believe in staying together for a child's sake. That never ends well."

She clamped her bottom lip between her teeth and bit hard, quelling the words she wanted to say. Once she'd gotten her emotions under control she said, "I'm not moving to Chicago. It'll be easier for you to see the baby if I'm here."

"Suit yourself." He halted. "I have to meet the guys for a study session, so I'll see you next week." Without so much as a wave, he spun and walked away, not even bothering with a glance over his shoulder.

Tiffany sighed and glanced down at the listing clenched in her hands. As much as his actions and words hurt, one thought rose to the top of the pile. Aiden had purchased a penthouse in Chicago. That gave her hope. The man was planning their future. Perhaps he was gravitating toward her without even realizing it.

Time to practice patience and let it happen. In the end, he'd return to her as he always did. She didn't kid herself that he'd remained celibate during three years of overseas travel, and she'd welcomed him with open arms after that separation. She'd do it one last time and then hold him close forever.

In the meantime, she needed to check out the competition for her husband's affections. Now she knew the woman's full name and where she lived, it wouldn't take long to discover the details. Angelica Giannelli. New York City.

Chapter 23

Aiden

Every day felt like a marathon to Aiden. Especially on the days he attended the doctor's appointments and fought the tumultuous mixture of emotions coursing through him. Now they'd passed the danger zone and were heading into the second trimester of Tiffany's pregnancy, the time had come to make solid plans for the future.

Tiffany hadn't embraced his suggestion about Chicago, but he'd keep working to convince her that his solution was sound. The rundown penthouse had caught his eye one weekend when Tom had invited him along on a house-hunting trip.

The apartment looked rough, but Aiden saw past the stained harvest-gold shag carpets, the ancient olive-green appliances, and the worn fixtures. Hidden underneath were solid structural bones and to his surprise, spectacular hardwood floors. It would double as a great investment and the home he felt obligated to provide for Tiffany and the baby.

The bleat of his phone brought him back to the present.

"Hi, honey. Do you have time for a visit this weekend?"

Aiden thought of the heavy study sessions he should attend, but the thought of spending time with Angelica was enticing.

"I'm invited to a dinner party on Saturday night. You could be my date," she said.

"Sounds like fun. I'll drive up this afternoon." He glanced at his watch. If he packed and hit the road within the hour, he could be in New York before dark.

"Lovely. That will give us some time to relax. I'll text you my home address. You'll stay with me this weekend."

"You've finally decided I'm not a crazy stalker, huh?"

"I always knew that, but we should stop lurking in the various hotels around New York. Time for you to meet my friends."

He frowned at this proclamation but reminded himself that she knew the score. It wasn't a secret that his marriage had recently met its demise, even if she still didn't know his actual age or much about his friends and family. Anyway, enjoying a relationship with no strings attached could only be viewed as a healthy first step to recovery.

Once he'd hung up his phone, he headed for home. His footsteps grew a touch lighter as he considered spending the weekend with Angelica.

After a quick text to Will and Matthias to let them know he'd be out of town and would miss Friday classes, he packed a bag and tossed it in the trunk of his car. He'd make up the study time next week. Right now he needed to blow off some steam after the tense afternoon with his soon-to-be-ex-wife.

Aiden woke Friday morning to an empty space beside him in Angelica's bed. He stretched, a smile twitching at his lips as moments later, the woman appeared in the doorway carrying two steaming cups.

"Morning, my love," she said as she sashayed across the floor and offered him one of the mugs before positioning herself cross-legged on the bed beside him.

"I figured you'd gone to work," he said as he propped himself against the puffy pillows.

"No, I arranged to work from home today. I got up early to answer my emails and reschedule all of today's phone conferences to Monday. It was a lovely treat for you to arrive last night, and I thought we'd spend the day together."

Aiden sipped his coffee and sighed in contentment. "Sounds great. What did you have planned?"

A sly grin appeared. "You don't know?" She wiggled her brows and set her cup aside before retrieving his and placing it beside hers. "It's been two weeks since I last saw you, so figured I would take advantage of the situation." Angelica rose to her knees and slung her leg across him, caressing his lips with hers while trickling a finger down his bare chest.

Aiden tangled a hand into her thick wild waves and returned the kiss. Spending the day lounging in bed with a beautiful woman could only help repair his shattered life.

Hours later, Aiden joined Angelica in the kitchen, leaning against the counter and sipping red wine as she donned an apron.

"Uh-uh," she said as she claimed the glass from his hand and drained the last of the liquid. "No loitering allowed. I'll teach you to make Nonna's famous risotto and rack of lamb."

Aiden laughed and poured more wine, handing it to Angelica before he located another glass for himself. Then he rolled up his sleeves and permitted her to order him around the kitchen as he memorized the recipe. Most of the meals they'd shared had been in small out of the way bistros or hotel room service shared in bed. Cooking a meal and seeing her comfort level in the kitchen made the woman even more appealing.

"You're rather good at this chef stuff." Angelica set the rack of lamb aside to rest before she wrapped an arm around his waist and peered into the pan of risotto. "You'd almost think you'd made this before."

"Once or twice." Aiden lifted one shoulder as he gave the rice another gentle stir and adjusted the gas flame underneath the pan. "I love to cook, but I don't get the opportunity these days."

"Why is that?" She set two shallow bowls on the counter. "You've never said much about your life in Philly." A smile twitched the corner of her lips. "My sources haven't turned up much dirt on Aiden from Philadelphia."

He shot a look her way. "You've been checking up on me?"

"Sounds like I'm the crazy stalker, right?" She shrugged. "It does make me wonder why you are so secretive when you know so much about me." One of her hands rose, her flattened palm toward him. "No strings attached. That is what we agreed. But I would like to know something about the man who is sharing my bed. Even what it is you do would be a great start."

"I'm a medical student at the University of Pennsylvania."

"Now was that so hard?" Angelica pressed a kiss to his cheek. "So it will be Dr. Hamilton someday soon." She tapped a fingertip against pursed lips. "I'd bet Philly isn't your home town. That's why I am having a tough time finding information."

He scoffed. "Like you couldn't hire someone to dig up everything including the color of my damn underwear."

"I'm privy to that information, honey." Her light laugh made him smile. "I didn't want to treat you like a criminal. What I would like is for you to open up and share a few tiny details about your life."

Aiden flicked off the burner and portioned the risotto into the bowls before adding a sprinkle of cheese and the lightly roasted asparagus spears. "I'm terrible at sharing. Besides, you won't like what you learn."

"Are you a criminal? Or are you still living with your wife and I'm slotted into the role of mistress? Or are you an underachiever living in a hovel on the wrong side of the tracks?"

With a shake of his head, he said, "I'm a guy whose wife cheated on him while he busted his ass studying to be a doctor." He lifted his glass and gulped a mouthful of wine. "My life is sad and pathetic, though spending my time in your company is the exception to that rule."

"I'm sorry, Aiden. My husband did the same to me. It went on for months before I learned the truth. Like a stupid needy woman, I forgave him after he said he'd ended it and took him back. Only a few weeks later, I found out he'd never stopped seeing her. So I showed him the door."

He reached over and took her hand. "It hurts. I'm sorry that happened to you, Angie."

"Well, no matter. I'm over it. Let's stop with the depressing talk and enjoy our dinner." She patted his arm as she rose and headed toward the kitchen.

Aiden knew the time of revelation was coming. He just didn't know when or how.

∼

Saturday dawned bright and sunny, so when Angelica suggested a stroll in Central Park, Aiden agreed. He loved the wide open spaces amidst the crowded bustle of the city.

With their hands linked, they wandered along one of the many pathways as she filled him in on a few of the details about the friends he'd meet that evening. At eleven, they stopped for an early lunch at her favorite Manhattan bistro, followed by a visit to a local wine shop.

"I forgot to pick up a small gift for the hostess." Angelica selected an expensive bottle of red wine. "Marissa isn't much of a cook, but she has exquisite taste in pretty much everything else."

Aiden grimaced. "So I need to be prepared to eat little and hide bits in my napkin?"

Angelica snickered and gave him a playful poke in the ribs. "Somehow I can't picture you doing that. But never fear. She has an accomplished caterer who takes care of the food for all of her dinner parties." She tilted her head to look up at him. "I should have reminded you to bring a suit."

"I brought one. You said dinner party, and I wasn't sure of the dress code."

The woman gave him an appraising look. "You aren't just some medical student from Philly, are you, Aiden?" Her gaze traveled over him. "The first night I met you, you were dressed well, but the clothes were rather nondescript. Every time since, you look more like a GQ model than a starving student. And the car isn't some over-priced lease to pick up woman, is it?"

"I never said I was starving." He held the door as they exited onto the street.

"Where did you grow up?"

"Chicago."

Angelica pulled him to a halt and turned to face him. "Your name is Hamilton and you're from Chicago?" Her eyes narrowed as she slid a hand up his chest. At the last second, she snagged the wallet out of his inner jacket pocket.

"Angie, don't." Aiden tried to catch her hand, but she stepped back.

"What are you hiding?" She tipped her head downward but kept peering up at him as she opened it.

Aiden shoved his hands into his pockets and bowed his own head, watching her from the corner of his eye as she sorted through his leather wallet, first inspecting his everyday credit card and debit card. She'd seen those multiple times when he'd picked up the tab for lunch or a hotel.

After tucking them in their slots, she ruffled the stack of bills. "Nope, not starving." The next item she came across was his platinum unlimited credit card given to him by his grandmother. "Well, well. Not everyone gets one of these." She held it between her fingertips as she located his driver's license. The furrow between her eyes deepened.

"Angie—"

She squinted in his direction before she studied his picture. "Aiden James Thomas Franklin Hamilton. Birthdate …" Angelica shook her head as she returned his credit card and ID to his wallet and came up with the photo. "This is her, right? She's lovely." A thoughtful look appeared as she flipped it over. "All my love, Tiffany."

At least Angelica hadn't found the other item he'd tucked in there, but she might if she kept digging. He reached for his wallet just as her fingers connected with the paper.

"What is this?" She peered at the picture. "Is this what I think it is?" Angelica's eyes shimmered as she placed the image inside and shoved the wallet at him. "You lied. You're barely legal. You certainly shouldn't be hanging out in bars and drinking. I could be disbarred for providing you alcohol." Her sharp inhale sounded like a hiss. "But the biggest disappointment is learning you're running around on your pregnant wife."

"No. Well, yes, she's pregnant. But it's not like that."

"Famous last words." She spun and strode away, the heels of her boots clicking against the sidewalk.

Aiden tucked his wallet into his pocket and jogged after her. "Angie. Wait." He caught her arm as he fell into step beside her. "We're separated. And I never lied about my age. You assumed it."

Angelica barely faltered as she passed the doorman on the way into her building with Aiden on her heels. Silence reigned for the entire ride to her penthouse apartment. The moment the door opened, she said, "Pack your things." Her boot hit the floor with a thunk. "Go home to your pregnant wife." The second boot followed the first. Angelica disappeared toward the kitchen, her exit followed by the rattle of ice and the distinctive clink of glassware.

Aiden wasn't sure what to do. Part of him longed to follow and explain, but the larger part of him had already given up. What was the point? She obviously didn't care what he had to say, so he headed toward the bedroom to do as she requested. Pack and get the hell out.

He located his bag in her walk-in closet and set it on the bed.

"Why did you lie?"

Aiden scarcely looked her way as he stowed items in his suitcase. "I never lied even if I omitted a few details. Tiffany cheated and we're separated. The kid may or may not be mine. I am a medical student. And yeah, I'm twenty, not twenty-five as you assumed. Whatever. I'm going."

"You missed the part where you're ADA James Hamilton's son." She crossed the room and placed a hand on his arm. "Is that true about the baby?"

"None of it matters."

"I'm sorry I overreacted." She sat on the bed and patted the space beside her. When he didn't respond, she tugged on his arm until he complied. "I like you, Aiden, but this thing we have will never work. I'm almost thirty-four and looking for more than you can give." The woman rested her hand on his knee and squeezed.

"What are you looking for? A husband? A white picket fence? Kids?"

"No." She shook her head. "That's a little too suburban housewife for me. I want an equal partner who isn't afraid of my success. Most men can't handle a strong woman, but you seemed different. Except you're twenty and only beginning your journey. How can I expect you to make such decisions and sacrifices?"

"You think I'm too young for you."

"That's a fact, not an opinion." She slid an arm around his waist and leaned into him. "You're also still in love with your wife and this child she's carrying. You, my love, want to be a father."

"And how do you figure that?"

"There's a lingering sadness when you talk about her. And you carry a picture of her and an ultrasound of the baby in your wallet. When is she due?"

"September," he said. "Problem is, she doesn't know whose kid it is. I caught her cheating and a few weeks later she made the announcement about the baby."

Angelica tightened her embrace. "So now you wait until you can do DNA testing?"

"I wish it were that easy. The other guy walked. I'm married to her." He shrugged.

"You won't fight it in court?"

"To what end?" Aiden dragged in a long breath and closed his eyes. "Every time I hear that tiny heartbeat and see the pictures on the screen, I fall a little more in love. I'm a stupid, gullible idiot for letting her drag me into this. I've tried and failed to keep it under control."

"No. You're a sweet, loving man who can't walk away even given the circumstances. That shows a strength I wish more men had." Angelica patted his cheek. "How long was the affair going on?"

"She says it was one time and that it was a mistake."

"Do you believe her?"

"I don't know. I guess I want to, but how do I ever trust her again after that? We've been through so much loss and pain." He blinked hard and covered his face with his hands. "Stupid me. I never saw it coming."

"Do we ever? When we truly love someone we see their best and accept their worst." Her warm arms wrapped around him and she pulled his head to rest on her shoulder, stroking his hair. "Deciding to be this child's father, regardless of biology, is a brave choice."

A choked sob escaped him. It didn't amount to a choice at all. Deep inside, he longed for the daughter they'd been forced to give away. His little girl was never far from his thoughts, especially these days. "It's not brave. It's selfish."

"Why would you ever say that?" She pressed a kiss to his temple.

Aiden clung to this woman who offered him a level of compassion that had been so rare in his life. "We had a baby girl. We were forced to give her up for adoption. She's five now and I've never even seen her. This baby is our second chance." He buried his head against her neck, waiting for her reaction to this secret. Very few people knew about their daughter; they'd never told a single one of their friends.

"Oh, honey. You and Tiffany have been through more than I imagined." Angelica sighed. "I want to hate her for hurting you, but how can I judge a young woman who's been forced into giving up her child? How old was she then?"

"Fifteen. And I know what you're going to say. We were too young. It's all for the best. Our daughter was adopted and now she has parents who love her better than we ever could." He hoped his words were true and his baby girl had been welcomed into a loving, happy family who gave her everything he'd never had.

"I'd never say or even think anything of the sort." She pressed her palms against his cheeks and forced him to look into her eyes. "It's clear you love this woman more than you're willing to admit even to yourself. She hurt you," Angelica said as she pressed a flattened palm directly over his heart, "but you should do your best to forgive her. Go home and work on your marriage. Be a proper father to this child. Otherwise, you'll have regrets."

"Take her back?" Aiden shook his head. "She slept with someone else."

Angelica frowned. "Don't you dare play that double-standard bullshit card. How many times have you been in bed with another woman since you found out? And even more to the point, how long did it take you to commit that first transgression after you discovered her cheating? How many women have you been with since you left your wife?"

He couldn't bear to look her in the eye. This woman had him all figured out. "Who says she even wants me back?"

"That guilty expression on your face tells me we're circling the truth. I'd bet she's already asked but you're so wrapped up in your own anger and pain you refused her."

Aiden rubbed at his face with one hand, keeping his head down.

"Does she know about me?"

He nodded and closed his eyes.

"And she still wants you to come home?" Angelica asked. "And just how did she learn about your extracurricular activities?"

"Stop cross-examining me." Aiden glared at her.

"Occupational hazard." She rose and headed for the door. "Finish packing and I'll walk you out."

"What about the dinner party?"

"I'll manage, just like I have since my husband broke my heart." She glanced over her shoulder. "I have higher hopes for you and your marriage. You owe it to her to at least try, Aiden."

Aiden rose after she'd disappeared down the hallway. It seemed this, whatever it was, happened to be over. It saddened him as he'd loved the time he'd spent with this woman, but a glimmer of hope ignited as he thought of another woman who waited for him in Philadelphia.

A flicker of hope followed by a deluge of doubt. Was it a sign he'd become as guilty as Tiffany when he found solace in another woman's arms? Was Angelica right? Did he owe his wife the opportunity to explain her side and find a way to forgive her? Was he denying his true feelings?

And then he understood the truth. He'd traveled in an endless circle, finishing right back where he started. Completely in love with the girl who'd captured his heart at the age of thirteen.

He gathered the last of his belongings and carried his bag to the door.

Angelica appeared a moment later. "Ready?" At his nod, she wrapped her arms around him. "I'll miss you, but this is for the best. We could never work in the long-term." She cupped his face in her hands and placed a kiss on his lips. "Take care of yourself, Aiden."

"You too, Angie." After one last hug, he stepped into the elevator. There was no point in prolonging their final goodbye.

Chapter 24

Tiffany

Tiffany slung her purse onto the chair beside the door before collapsing onto the couch. The trip from Philly to New York and back had exhausted her. She rested one hand on her belly as she contemplated her next move. "Your daddy is in big trouble," she muttered as she massaged her side to ease the ache from hours in a car.

Her initial research had revealed that Aiden's mistress was a high-powered lawyer. A beautiful, thirty-something, successful woman who she'd tracked to a swanky Manhattan address in a building overlooking Central Park.

The worst moment had been watching Angelica emerge this morning, all smiles as she gazed up at the dark-haired man on her arm. Nothing could have prepared Tiffany to see her husband holding hands and cuddling with this stunning woman after spending the night in said woman's bed.

That gut-wrenching sight was followed by an awful, heart-stopping moment when Angelica stared across the street to the spot Tiffany stood. The slight smirk and toss of the woman's silky mane of hair issued a silent challenge as their eyes met. *Just try to take him back, blondie.*

Tiffany had hurried away, stopping under the cover of some bushes to spy as the couple headed into the park.

The realization she was competing with the sexy older woman for her husband's affection overwhelmed her. Enticing him to return home might be impossible. However, she'd take whatever he dished out and continue to remind herself what, and who, had caused this unhappy situation.

That Aiden agreed to support the child without a fight was a small measure of forgiveness in itself. Now her task was to prove she loved him and do whatever he demanded in order to win him back.

Tiffany rose from the couch, wincing as pain streaked down her side. She closed her eyes and took several deep breaths. A familiar ache set in, reminding her of her first pregnancy and how her body changed to accommodate the new life inside her. This was a normal part of the change. Within the next few weeks, she'd feel the first stirrings of life and they'd be allowed to find out if she was carrying a son or a daughter.

She choked out a sob and pressed her flattened palm to her stomach. This child she'd never give up, no matter what happened between her and her husband. Her heart ached. It had once created joy to even think the magical title bestowed upon him, but now it only brought sorrow. She may have lost his love forever even if he was willing to participate in raising the baby.

As tired as she was, Tiffany sat on the stool in front of her art table. She closed her eyes and inhaled, forcing herself to focus and allow the pain the guide her fingers. The lines flowed onto the page and she lost track of time, fully absorbed in the art of creating. Until that moment when the softest of clicks made her aware she was no longer alone.

She threw a startled glance over her shoulder, her eyes widening at the sight of the man frozen in the middle of the room, his eyes downcast as if he lacked the will to take those final steps. The last person she expected to see in this apartment. "What are you doing here?"

He lifted his head only enough to peer at her through red-rimmed eyes before he shoved his hands into his jean pockets. His hair stuck out at odd angles, and a light stubble had appeared on his jawline. Aiden raised one shoulder in a tiny half-shrug.

To Tiffany, he was the most beautiful sight in the world, even with his rumpled clothes and unkempt appearance. "Say something," she whispered, rising to her feet and taking one small step toward him as her gaze fell to the overnight bag at his feet. Her pulse quickened as she absorbed what was happening.

His eyes closed as his head bowed again and he swallowed hard, the only other motion the gentle flutter of his eyelids.

The words locked in her throat as she forced herself into motion, one tiny step at a time. Tiffany had never seen him so close to the edge of tears. The man never cried. Ever. That he might be about to wrenched her heart, creating a longing to comfort the man she loved so desperately. After an eternity, she stopped in front of him, so close that she could feel the heat radiating from his trembling body.

Without a word, he enfolded her in his embrace, burying his head against the crook of her neck. With a tiny but sharp inhale, he pulled her closer, molding her body against the hard length of him.

A shiver coursed through her as she rested her head on his chest, listening to the solid but rapid thud of his heart while attempting the impossible feat of becoming part of him. She soaked up his warmth and his musky masculine tang, not speaking for fear of shattering the spell binding them together. Questioning what brought him here was unthinkable. She'd be thankful for his presence and hope this was their new beginning.

"I want to come home," he whispered.

Tiffany squeezed her eyes shut, but even so, the tear escaped and trickled down her cheek. She bobbed her head and lifted her chin, her lips seeking his, plundering their softness and reveling in the taste of him. The smell of him. She savored everything she'd thought was lost to her forever.

She felt weightless as he carried her to the bedroom and laid her on the bed, the solid weight of him pressing her into the mattress. Her fingers seemed to act of their own accord, undressing him, caressing his heated skin as she wrapped her limbs around him. If this was a dream, she never wanted to wake up.

Hours later, when her eyes fluttered open in the dim light of early morning, she was relieved to feel his warm naked body pressed against her back and his arm draped over her hip. She linked her fingers through his, a satisfied smirk touching her lips as she drew in a long, gentle breath, their combined scents tickling her nostrils. How she'd missed the mornings of cuddling like this with Aiden.

He dropped a kiss to her hair, the gentle pressure of his fingers signaling he too was awake.

She rolled over and placed a hand against his cheek, studying him as she absorbed the fact he was truly back where he belonged. In their bed.

"I have something for you." He reached over the side, coming up with a bag.

The sight of the familiar logo made her smile. She dipped her hand inside, her fingers wrapping around the soft texture of the plush stuffed bunny's ear as she pulled it free and hugged it to her chest. "It's adorable, Aiden. I love it."

"It's for the baby. There's more."

She peered inside, finding a magazine. "What is this?" Her breath caught as she realized it was a catalogue full of choices for decorating a nursery.

"Sorry, I didn't have time to wrap it, but I figured we should order the furniture."

This may be a small peace offering, but she took it as a sign of her husband's commitment—or acceptance—of his impending fatherhood. But still, a thought intruded into her bliss. Yesterday morning he'd woken in someone else's arms. Angelica's arms. That moment when the other woman's eyes met hers replayed in her mind.

"What?" he asked in a low voice. "Why are you looking at me like that?"

"Nothing." She forced a smile, blinking hard against the tears.

He scoffed. "That look isn't nothing, Tiff. Just say it and get it over with."

She clamped her lip between her teeth, hoping for some inspiration on how to approach the subject at the top of her mind.

Aiden sucked in a long breath but only rested his forehead against hers, one hand sliding downward, his fingertips skimming her navel before he cupped his palm over her flesh. A tentative touch reminiscent of another time and place, except back then he'd never hesitated to rub her belly and inquire about the baby she carried.

"How many?" she whispered. "I mean, I know about her. Angelica. But how many others were there?"

He drew back, a deep furrow appearing in his brow. "Can we not?"

"I need to know. Please. Just tell me."

"Does it make a difference?"

She gave a tiny nod, even though she was truly afraid of the answer. Perhaps her imagination had run wild and his answer would ease her worries. "I'll start. Only once. The one and only time you already know because it got us into this mess."

He stared at her, his lips set in a flat line. As hard as he tried to hide the truth, the flicker in his eyes told her the jab about women that day in the diner wasn't only about getting a reaction out of her. He'd played the field from the moment he walked out that door.

"How many, Aiden?"

He sat, swinging his feet to the floor with his back toward her and rubbing a hand over his face. "Don't do this."

She eyed the expanse of flesh, noting the streaks marring the smoothness. Had she done that? Or were those little red scratches from a night with one of his other women? With a fingertip, she traced across one of the marks, tears burning her eyes as he stiffened and pulled away.

Without a glance in her direction, he retrieved his clothing from the floor, tugging on his jeans first before working on his shirt buttons. "This was a mistake," he muttered.

Tiffany sat and hauled the covers under her armpits. "I don't have the right to ask about my husband's sex life?"

"It won't make things better or easier." He paused half-way to the door, his shoulders slumping. "At least you didn't have to watch."

"And you'll never let me forget it, will you? Forever I'll be the cheating wife."

"I didn't even bring it up." The slight scoff carried across the room as he turned, his lip curling. "You said you'd forgiven me. You said you wanted me to come home. I'm here. I'm trying to get over it, but nothing will ever be enough for you."

Her breath hitched as he retreated, his footsteps thudding on the stairs, followed by a brief silence and then a slamming door. She clamped her teeth on her lip, fighting the urge to rush after him. There was no point as he'd be half-way home before she managed to dress. Anyway, it would be best to give him plenty of space before she begged him to forgive her. Again.

If only she'd had enough sense to keep her stupid mouth shut. In mere seconds she'd broken her vow and simultaneously derail his reconciliation attempt. Aiden's pain and anger had resurfaced and were directed at her.

Tiffany rose from the bed and tugged a shirt over her head before doubling over in agony. The tortuous cramping was followed by a warm trickle running down her leg. A red droplet appeared on the hardwood by her feet. She swayed, battling lightheadedness as she crouched on the floor and wrapped an arm over her belly. The smear of blood on her thigh caused another wave of dizziness.

"No."

With shaking hands, she fumbled for the phone, dialing the familiar number by heart.

You've reached—

She stabbed at the disconnect and dialed again, tears flooding her eyes at the sound of the recorded greeting. There was no way he'd answer given his exit only minutes before. Her instinct took over as she did the next best thing and called for an ambulance, knowing she wouldn't manage the trip to the ER alone.

Tiffany curled into a ball, clutching her stomach as a nurse tucked a heated blanket around her.

"Are you sure I can't call someone?"

Tiffany sobbed. The only person she could think of was Aiden, but he wouldn't come. Not after how she'd behaved. Now she was being punished. "No."

"Press the call button if you need anything." The nurse offered a faint smile and adjusted the IV drip before leaving the room.

Her lids felt heavy and her eyes drifted closed as she tried to ignore the dull ache in her belly. The dose of pain medication gave her a fuzzy unfocused feeling and all she wanted to do was sleep.

What else was left aside from the awful devastation? The grim set of the doctor's lips as she performed an exam and ultrasound told Tiffany it was over. The empty words. *I'm sorry, there's no heartbeat.* Now Aiden would leave her forever. If it hadn't been for the baby, he would never have come home in the first place.

She floated in and out of consciousness, only vaguely aware of the hospital noises around her. A slight sound made her open her eyes, her gaze drawn to the man in the chair only feet from her bed. "Why are you here?" she whispered.

He lifted his head to stare at her with red bleary eyes which closed as he shook his head. "One of the nurses saw your name on the board," he said in a low, gravelly voice. "She called me." He rose, swaying as he moved toward her. "I'm sorry about the baby, Tiff."

The scent on his breath made her nose twitch. "How did that nurse have your number?" She narrowed her eyes. "You're wasted. How dare you show up drunk and pretend this means anything to you?"

He stopped inches short of the bed. "I came as soon as I—"

"You didn't need to. If I'd wanted you here, I would have phoned you. Tell your nosey little girlfriend to butt out."

"She's not—"

"Just go. Walk away like you always do. The baby's gone, and you're no longer obligated. Get out of my room." She wiggled onto her other side, presenting him with her back.

"You shouldn't be alone."

"Get out. I don't want you." A tear escaped and created a trail down her cheek, but she hid her face in her pillow, not wanting him to see. It would be best if he went now. Time she learned to exist without him.

Chapter 25

Aiden

AIDEN STARED AT HER BACK, longing to reach out, to hold her, to provide a thin bit of comfort in this moment of tragic loss and seek a little consolation of his own, but he didn't. Instead, he stumbled from the room, keeping his head down as he headed for the exit.

Tiffany no longer wanted him in her life. With the baby gone, she had no reason to keep him around or forgive him. Their last connection had crumbled.

So he walked, forcing one foot after another, the pain of his own losses keeping pace. He'd never outrun this, and though the alcohol had taken off the edge, it made it close to impossible to string together a coherent thought. Finally, he sank onto a nearby bench and just sat, unable to move for the longest time. The child he'd allowed himself to fall in love with was gone. As was his marriage. Their cumulative mistakes had taken their toll.

There was nothing more he could do except walk away and give her back everything he'd stolen when he married her. He scrolled through the numbers on his phone and dialed, tapping one foot until she answered. "Michelle? Please don't hang up."

"Aiden? What's wrong? You sound funny."

"Tiffany needs you."

"What's happened?" A touch of panic infused her voice.

"She's in the hospital."

"Aiden, what's happening?"

"Please, please say you'll come." He sucked in a breath.

"David won't—"

"If you want your daughter back, get on the fucking plane."

"Do you mean …?"

"Yes," he whispered. "I'll give her the divorce. Now live up to your end."

"I'll be on the next flight." Silence hung for a moment. "She's my daughter. I love her."

Aiden cut the connection without uttering another word. He wished there was another option, but he was certain he could do nothing to help. At this moment, he was barely functioning or able to care for himself. Their relationship had reached the inevitable end and the best he could do was stay away.

He dragged himself to his feet and wandered aimlessly, ending up at his apartment. The silence of the small space didn't help, but he didn't feel like having company. He slid to the floor, propped himself against the wall and hugged his knees to his chest, staring blankly through the window.

Barely twenty-four hours ago, he'd harbored the hope that his marriage could be saved. Angelica had provided a persuasive argument, so despite the fact he'd spent a good portion of the weekend with the other woman, he'd made the bold move and shown up at the apartment.

He closed his eyes, the image of Tiffany's disgust imprinted forever in his mind. Her harsh questions about other women and the recrimination in her eyes as she voiced the question he most feared caused deep shame. Given the looks she shot his way, admitting to anything would be another huge mistake to add to the line of others already made.

It became evident that despite her claim she'd forgiven him, she hadn't and never would. Any errors in judgement he'd made during these short but volatile months would rise up and be used against him for eternity.

When the light dimmed and sufficient hours had passed, he dialed the number of the nurse who'd alerted him to Tiffany's admittance to the hospital. "It's Aiden. How's Tiffany doing?"

"As to be expected," Gina said. "She'll be here for a few days for monitoring, but it looks like she'll avoid any complications. How are you hanging in there?"

"I'll survive. Did Tiffany's mother show up?"

"Michelle Baxter? She arrived a couple of hours ago and has been a royal pain in the ass, so thanks for that."

"Sorry," he mumbled. "I didn't know who else to call."

"She'll be okay, Aiden. You take care of yourself and quit worrying."

"What about her room?" He pictured her in the double room, far away from the window. Tiffany loved to look outside and it always seemed to calm her. "Can you find a private one?"

Gina sighed. "Yes, but those are pricy. Her mother seems concerned about the hospital bill and I doubt she'd allow it."

"I'll cover it. Just get her moved, please? I'll settle the account, but don't mention it to either of them. Make something up."

"You've got it. Call me if you need to talk."

"I owe you one." After he disconnected the call, he returned to his own contemplation of the view through the glass.

Michelle had kept her promise. And now he'd keep his.

———

The next days passed in a blur. He spent the majority of his time curled up in bed, fighting the exhaustion he couldn't seem to shake.

"Hey," a deep voice said as the intruder shook his shoulder. "Wake up."

He opened his eyes, the familiar face coming into focus. "How the hell did you get in here without a key?"

"I have my ways." Tom sat on the edge of the bed. "I thought you knew better than to drop out of communication after that last bullshit disappearing act you pulled."

"It's not disappearing if you never leave your apartment."

"It is when nobody has seen or heard from you in days. Will seemed to think you were in New York, but Angelica said you were in Philly. She believes you're home making up with your wife." His brows rose. "You look like hell and Tiffany isn't answering my calls, so I guess that's delusional thinking."

"You called Angie?" Aiden shifted into an upright position and accepted the glass of water his friend held out.

"I figured it was worth a try. So what's happening? Returning to the love nest didn't go so well?"

Aiden shook his head. "Tiffany lost the baby."

"Damn. I'm sorry. Is she okay?"

"She ended up in the hospital but she'll be fine. I guess I'm off the hook." He forced a smile.

"Don't be an asshole." His friend gave him a death stare. "Get your ass out of bed. I don't care what the circumstances, you should be there. You can't leave her in the hospital alone."

"She's not alone. Michelle flew in from Chicago." Aiden shrugged. "I was told in no uncertain terms to get the hell out, so I'll stay away."

"So that's it?"

"It was a simple exchange. Michelle promised to take care of her if I agreed to vanish from her daughter's life. It's what they've always wanted. Me, only a distant memory."

"And Angelica?"

"That's over. She didn't love my secrets and kicked me out."

"Go shower and we'll get out of this apartment. I refuse to let you withdraw from the real world."

Aiden nodded, knowing it was useless to argue. The man would force him back to reality, no matter whether he wanted to be there or not.

Aiden returned to class the next day after reassuring Tom he'd be fine and sending his friend home to New Haven. Whatever happened, he'd been enough of a burden and taken up too much of Tom's time.

He struggled to engage in the discussions and decided to skip the study session and head home. He'd arrived at the apartment and unpacked his bag when someone knocked on his door. "Michelle," he said. "What are you doing here?"

She stepped forward and wrapped her arms around him. "I'm sorry," she whispered. "I didn't even know you two were expecting a baby." A sniffle broke free as she released him and brushed at her eyes.

He motioned her inside. "Is she okay?"

"She's been released from the hospital. I packed her personal belongings and the movers picked everything up this afternoon. We're in a hotel tonight and we'll fly home tomorrow." Michelle sighed and dangled the keyring. "She didn't want to stay in the apartment even for a night. I thought you should have these back. All the furniture is still there."

Aiden accepted the keys but said nothing. He'd never live in the apartment he'd shared with his wife. The memories associated with that place would be overwhelming.

"Thank you for calling. It's best she come home where I can take care of her. She's so thin and does nothing but cry."

The pang hit him straight in the chest. The hug may have been genuine, but the words and accompanying glare placed a bundle of guilt directly on his shoulders.

"She'll be much happier at home in her own bed. Once she's ready, she can return to school."

"I'll pay her tuition and—"

"No, no." Michelle gave a vigorous head shake. "All we need is for you to file and pay for the divorce. She'll expect nothing else. Just keep your promise and let her go." She offered a tight smile. "David needs time to warm up to the idea she's moving home so it will be easier if you keep your distance."

"Can you at least let me know how she's doing?"

"Let me worry about my daughter, Aiden. She's no longer your responsibility."

Aiden held back the derisive snort. "Make a clean break so she can get on with her life."

"I'm glad you understand and are on board." Michelle patted his arm. "In a few months, it will be like it never happened." The woman straightened and focused her gaze on him. "I trust you will keep this confidential. It will be easier for my daughter to move forward if this little incident isn't publicized."

"Is that all?" He glanced at his watch, eager to have this woman out of his apartment. "I have somewhere to be."

The hug she offered was tolerated because he didn't feel he had a choice. Pushing the woman away would accomplish nothing and make it impossible to approach her in the future.

This awkward and difficult situation was of his own making. Now he'd learn to live with it. Watching his dreams of the future fade into nothingness was almost more than he could bear, but maybe that was what you did for those you loved. Let them find the happiness they deserved without you.

Aiden waited for two days before he faced the hurdle of dealing with the apartment. He couldn't risk running into Michelle or even worse, Tiffany. The end of their relationship carried a rawness and seeing her would rip open the wound that hadn't yet begun to heal.

He entered the silent apartment, closing his eyes for a moment, hoping to reclaim memories of better time, finding nothing but ghosts flitting through his mind. He shook it off and wandered across the room, stopping to run a hand over Tiffany's art table, saddened that the gift had been deemed unworthy of making the trip to Chicago. With one finger, he slid the top drawer open. Empty.

He made a brief stop in the kitchen and found the cupboards much as they had been the day he moved in, complete with the dishes, except for Tiffany's favorite coffee mug. At the bottom of the stairs, he stopped with one hand resting on the bannister and bowed his head, fighting the murky flashes of raging battles and hurtful words.

After some time, he forced himself to mount the stairs, one slow step at a time. The office was empty except for the desk and chair. The second bedroom had several bags and boxes stowed in the closet. He peered inside, cringing at the sight of the pile of tiny sleepers and receiving blankets.

Other various baby items were stacked inside the next box; an unopened musical mobile, a set of colorful blocks, and an activity mat along with books about baby development and milestones. Tucked down the side, he found the catalogue he'd given her the morning after his return from New York. His vision blurred at the array of decorating ideas and furniture for the perfect nursery. Ideas and furniture that would never be used for their child.

He turned away. No point in dwelling on what would never be. Fate had decided they wouldn't parent a child. At least not together.

A small open box sat on the bed in the master bedroom, the ornaments he'd given Tiffany to commemorate their Christmas celebrations nestled inside. He didn't dwell on those as a smeared patch of red on the hardwood captured his attention. *Blood.* He lowered himself onto the edge of the bed, fixated on the spot as another wave of guilt washed over him.

She'd called not long after he left that final morning, but awash in his own anger, he'd ignored his phone. Instead of answering and trying to work things out or coming to her aid, he'd turned to his usual crutch and spent the next few hours drinking. By the time Gina had reached him, it was all over. Tiffany hadn't cared that he'd rushed to be by her side, but why would she? With the baby gone, he was of no further use to her.

Unworthy. He wasn't fit to be a husband or a father. The spectacular failure to provide Tiffany the love and security she needed loomed over him. His time and energy had been devoted to the pursuit of his career as a doctor, and now, that was all he had left.

Chapter 26

Tiffany

TIFFANY STARED OUT THE WINDOW, fighting the tears burning behind her eyes as the sedan turned into the driveway of the familiar home. She clutched the soft caramel-colored bunny in her arms, unable to let it go. It had taken many tears and a huge argument with her mother, but in the end, she'd won out and kept it.

"Welcome home, honey," her mother said as she patted Tiffany's knee.

Home. That wasn't a term she thought she'd be saying anytime soon in reference to Chicago. Not without her husband, but that dream shattered the moment her mother darkened the door of her hospital room. Her parents would have nothing to do with her unless Aiden had forsaken her and the life they'd planned.

Her mother chattered on as the driver unloaded their suitcases and carried them into the front hall, leaving with a generous tip.

Tiffany peered up the staircase, hoping she could escape to her bedroom without having to deal with her father. All she wanted to do was crawl into her bed and sleep.

"Tiffany?"

"I'm tired. Can I just go to bed?"

"Oh." A slight frown appeared. "It's only the middle of the afternoon, but I suppose a nap wouldn't hurt you. I'll wake you in time for dinner."

Tiffany carried her bag upstairs, each step feeling like another nail in the coffin. Now she was back, would she ever be allowed to leave?

Except for the pile of boxes stacked against one wall, her room was the same as when she'd left. The bed was made up with the same duvet and the same pictures hung on the wall. She pulled back the covers and stepped out of her clothes, dropping them in a pile on the floor before climbing between the sheets, the stuffed toy cradled against her chest.

She curled in a ball and closed her eyes, willing it all away. The empty ache in her belly felt like it might never cease.

"Wake up."

Tiffany forced her eyes open and peered at her mother looming over the bed.

"Your father is home. Get up and join us for dinner."

She shook her head and burrowed under the covers. "I'm tired. Let me sleep."

"No, it's time to rejoin the land of the living." Her mother drew back the covers, a sigh escaping as she stared at her daughter. "Aren't you a bit old to be sleeping with stuffed animals?" With a firm tug, she freed the bunny from Tiffany's grasp and tossed it onto the dresser. "You're skin and bones."

Tiffany reached for the covers, intending to haul them over her exposed body, but her mother waggled one of her old bathrobes in the air.

"I'll draw a bath. Up you get." She held the robe out, clearly intending to dress her daughter in it no matter the objections.

Tiffany sat on the edge of her mattress and suffered in silence as her mother guided her arms into the sleeves. Then the woman insisted on helping to her feet and tying the belt. "I'm not an invalid, Mother." Immediately, she felt sorrow as her mother blinked at her with shimmering eyes. "I'm sorry. I'm all hormonal."

Michelle gave her a sad smile and patted her arm. "It's fine, honey. You've been through an ordeal but I just want to take care of you. You're my baby girl." Her hand rose to cover her mouth as she emitted a small gasp. "Oh, sweetheart, I shouldn't have said that."

Tiffany bowed her head. "I'll fill my own bathtub." She hurried to the bathroom and closed the door, grateful to be alone as the tears poured down her cheeks. Her heart had broken yet again. Even if her mother meant well, it didn't make it any easier to be reminded not only the child she'd just lost, but the one that came before. Her own baby girl who'd been stolen from her arms only moments after birth.

The days dragged on, and to Tiffany, it felt like a return to her teenage years. She could barely breathe in the stifling atmosphere of her parents' home. They monitored her every move, her mother shuttling her to and from doctor's appointments but refusing to allow Tiffany use of the car. In Philly, they'd only had one, but Aiden had never refused access to the keys. This complete removal of personal freedom to come and go at will was difficult.

On top of that, her bank card and the joint credit card had gone missing from her wallet, and her phone was nowhere to be found. She could only assume Aiden had asked for them to be returned. Without access to their joint account, she'd become penniless, her last tiny pay check from the gallery spent long ago. She hadn't worked there since the night with Derrick.

All she wanted to do now was sleep, but her mother insisted on waking her early every morning and dragging her downstairs to force breakfast on her.

"You're too thin." Her mother tapped a finger against her pursed lips. "Eat a few more bites."

"I'm not hungry." Tiffany pushed a piece of pancake around with her fork. Even the three slices of crispy bacon failed to tempt her. With a sigh, she rose and crept up the stairs, intent on hiding under her covers.

"Where are you going?" The firm and demanding voice halted her in her tracks.

"For a nap." She hung her head, refusing to look at the man who blocked the top of the stairs.

"All you've done since you returned home is mope. Get yourself into the shower, dress, and find something productive to do." Her father scowled as she squeezed by. "This ridiculous behavior needs to stop immediately."

"I don't feel well," she whispered.

"Look at me, little girl," he said in a deep commanding voice. "You're lucky we've taken you in. Show some appreciation for our sacrifices."

She lifted her head enough to peer at him, wishing to be anywhere but here. The magnitude of her mistakes was crushing. Debilitating. Her heart ached as she thought of the children she'd lost and the man who'd left, abandoning her to this fate. The husband who'd found solace in another's arms and was probably with that other woman right now.

"Your poor mother is suffering from stress. She's taking pills to sleep at night because she's continuously worrying about you."

"Sorry," she muttered. After a small nod in his direction, she shuffled to the bathroom. Arguing was pointless. Her father would never understand how it felt to be her. To be unloved and unwanted by not only her parents, but by the man who'd promised to love her forever. To be the burden nobody wanted but still felt obligated to support. The door shut behind her with a soft click and she slid to the floor in a heap, curling into a ball and wrapping her arms around her knees. Continual shivers sped through her and her heart fluttered. It felt like she might die. What would be the difference if she did? Maybe it would put everyone out of their misery.

"Honey?" Her mother tapped on the door. "Your father has gone to work, and I have to run to the store, but I'll only be a few minutes. If you bathe and dress, we could go for a walk later."

She cleared her throat. "Okay." The faint sound of the front door closing prodded her into action. She dragged herself to her feet and peered into the hallway, listening for any sound. Greeted by the complete and refreshing silence, she tiptoed down the hall to the master bedroom.

The first spot she thought to look was in the small table on her mother's side of the king-sized four-poster bed. She poked through the drawer. *Nothing.* Her second thought was of the well-stocked cabinet in their bathroom. *Bingo.* Several small prescription bottles were lined up on the glass shelves. Her fingers trembled as she inspected the labels. One benefit of hanging around medical students while they studied was she'd overheard plenty about drugs and their various uses. Her eyes widened at the stockpile of powerful drugs at her mother's fingertips.

When she found the ones she wanted, she emptied the container into the palm of her hand, staring at them for a moment before tossing them into her mouth. She chased them down with a handful of water before doing the same with the second bottle. Then she snapped the caps on and replaced them neatly on the shelf.

This wasn't a desperate cry for help as some of Aiden's study group had asserted. She didn't want anybody to save her. There'd be no pill bottle lying beside her outstretched hand as a clear indication of what she'd done. By the time her mother discovered the missing drugs, it would be far too late. By then, Tiffany would be oblivious and the concerns of this world would no longer be hers. Aiden would be free to live his life without her.

She took her time, trailing her fingertips along the wall as she drifted toward her room, the sensation of floating taking over as her vision grew cloudy. The images drifted through her mind as she reclined on her bed. Aiden ... her last thoughts would be of the man she loved who no longer loved her. She closed her eyes, welcoming the peace that stole over her. *I'm sorry. I love you ...*

The steady beep irritated her, like the annoying buzz of a mosquito just out of swatting range. Her eyelids fluttered, a stark white ceiling barely coming into focus before the heaviness dragged her under again. Vague blips of sounds dug into her subconscious as a hand grasped her wrist followed by a fingertip forcing one eyelid upward. The bright light made her cringe.

"Tiffany?" The deep male voice asked. "Wake up for me, Tiffany. Can you open your eyes?"

"…is she …?" The voice faded in and out. A familiar voice. Her mother's voice.

Tiffany struggled to lift her arms but was unable to do so. Her body felt like a chunk of lead, weighted down and lethargic.

"That's it. Open those lovely blue eyes." The masculine voice accompanied a squeeze to her hand.

She exhaled and allowed herself to sink into the abyss. Even contemplating consciousness exhausted her.

When she eventually opened her eyes again, the same bland white expanse extended above her. She sighed and lifted her hand, grimacing at the sharp pain.

"You're awake. Don't move around too much, you'll pull out your IV." Her mother hovered over her, peering into Tiffany's eyes. "Do you know who I am?"

"You think I don't know my own mother?" Tiffany muttered, which led to a fit of coughing. Her throat was dry and raw, and her mouth pasty.

Michelle's lip quivered as she pressed the call button looped over the side of the bedrail. "So much for gratitude. Good thing I forgot my wallet, or it would have been too late. How do you think it made me feel to find my daughter …?" She issued a loud sniffle.

Tiffany turned her head away, a tear escaping and trickling down her cheek. She'd failed and nothing had changed. It was always about how she'd let her parents down, how much they'd suffered, and the disappointment she'd caused them.

"I brought this. I know how much you love it."

A soft bit of fluff tickled Tiffany's fingers as her mother lifted her hand. Despite her misery, she tucked the bunny against her chest and closed her eyes. Nothing would bring them back, so she'd accept the small comfort it provided.

"I tried to call Aiden—"

"Don't you dare tell him." She directed her gaze at her mother. "My welfare is none of his concern. He's made that very clear."

"He might be able to help."

"No. I don't ever want him to know. Keep your mouth shut for once. And get out of my room."

"Honey …" Her mother issued a deep sigh. "Get some sleep. You must be exhausted."

Tiffany rolled onto her side and closed her eyes, still clutching the stuffed toy. She wished everybody would just leave her alone.

Chapter 27

Aiden

The earth kept turning and life went on. At least that was Aiden's observation from behind his heavy lids as the professor droned on at the front of the class. His own personal misery meant nothing. It didn't matter that his wife had left. Nor did it matter that he'd lost two children in the short time he'd been alive. Everyone else went on while his world crumbled.

He propped his head against one hand and closed his eyes, sinking into a stupor as his phone vibrated in the side pocket of his bag. It had been bleating at him regularly, but he couldn't be bothered to even look. He didn't much care. Not about anything.

A jab in his ribs made him aware of the rustle of papers and the sound of zippers on bags as the rest of the class prepared to disburse.

"Wake up." Will shot him a concerned look. "It's time for our lab."

Aiden sighed as he wobbled to his feet, rubbing at his pounding temples. He shoved his laptop into his bag and slung it over his shoulder.

"You look like complete shit. Go home and sleep it off," his friend said in a low voice. "Why would you show up to class half-wasted? Do you want to screw up your career?"

He furrowed his brow and sent a bleary, questioning glance toward Will.

"I don't know who is worse, you or Matt. Both of you are totally losing it."

"Where is Matt anyway? I haven't seen him for days."

"He and Tess were at each other. They reconciled but then broke up again. Every time she pops up in his life, she ultimately dumps him, and he ends up hiding in his apartment for several days." Will's brows rose. "Sound like anyone you know?"

"Fuck off." Aiden glowered at the other man. "You don't have any clue what I'm dealing with."

"You're right, I don't. But you have to get it together, Aiden. Go and talk to someone and get your head on straight. I'm worried about you."

"Don't be. I'll be fine."

"Maybe, but this has been a stressful year and it's showing. Do I need to inform Tom?"

"Don't you dare. He already calls me daily for a pep-talk. The guy will fail all of his classes because of me."

"I hope he keeps after you until you pull your shit together. Now, answer your damn phone. It's driving me mad."

"Fine!" He waved a hand at his friend as he fished the mobile from his bag. The number on his call display made his stomach turn. "Michelle Baxter. Fabulous. Head to class, and I'll see what in the hell she wants."

Once Will had headed down the hall, Aiden found a bench and connected to his voice mail, a sick feeling building as he listened to the message. Michelle sounded panicked and made absolutely no sense with her rambles about Tiffany and pills. The ER.

He dialed Michelle's number, relieved when she answered right away.

"About time you called. Where have you been?"

"What happened to Tiffany? Is she okay? Do I need to come to Chicago?"

"It's under control, but you should know she overdosed on sleeping pills. I found her in time. But she doesn't want you here. She said I shouldn't even tell you, so keep this to yourself."

"Then why are you calling?" Aiden blinked hard at the familiar ache lodged in his chest. His wife was in pain and there was nothing he could do to make it better. There was no doubt in his mind that she'd demand he leave if he even tried to visit.

"It would be best if your lawyer prepared the divorce papers straight away. The sooner she puts this entire mess behind her, the better."

"But is she okay?" He gritted his teeth, holding back the scathing words he longed to direct at the woman. Now his wife had tried to off herself and the role of villain had been awarded to him. "Where did she get her hands on sleeping pills? We never kept drugs at the apartment."

"She's fine," Michelle said after a slight hesitation. "No damage done."

Aiden closed his eyes as he contemplated her useless words. The woman was in complete denial about her part in her daughters issues. "Were they yours?"

"How dare you blame me!"

"Get her some proper help, Michelle. Don't hide this away like you've done with everything else."

"Don't you dare tell me how to take care of my daughter! You have no business—"

"Whether you believe me or not, I want her to be happy. I've bowed out as you demanded. Now do your part and make sure this never happens again. Next time you might not be so lucky." After disconnecting the call, he dropped his head into his hands, fighting the urge to break down. He'd made a huge mistake in thinking the worst was over, only to be reminded that complacency was no answer. In his life, things could and would always get worse.

But what could he do? Tiffany wouldn't react well to his interference. No matter how hard it was, he had to learn to let go. If he ran to her aid this time, this dysfunctional mess of a marriage would drag him under when he was barely keeping it together.

For the next two days, he clung to the hope Michelle would take the necessary precautions to ensure her daughter's health and safety while battling the urge to board a Chicago bound plane. Instead of giving in to temptation, he contacted his lawyer and issued instructions for preparing the divorce documents.

On the third day, having heard nothing further from Michelle, he dragged himself out of bed and resigned himself to his fate as the youngest divorced guy around. He'd proven to be a complete and utter failure at marriage despite the promises he'd made to love Tiffany forever.

Now there was nothing to do but get on with his life. He trudged out the door, intent on keeping his promise to meet Will and Matthias for a study session. If he was late, Will would notify Tom and his friend would swoop down on him before lunchtime.

Not that he'd shared the latest development in his sad and pathetic life. That news would for sure capture Tom's attention and guarantee an immediate visit along with a long session where he'd be forced to talk when he had nothing left to say. It was easier to hold the pain close to his heart, allowing the familiar ache to remind him that loving any woman always led to disaster. Besides, telling any of their friends about Tiffany's situation would only give her an excuse to hate him more.

"You made it." Will nodded as Aiden arrived in front of the coffee shop where they often met to study. "Now we just have to locate Matthias."

"I left him a message, but he hasn't returned any calls."

"No, he's been elusive." Will glanced at his watch. "He's late. We should grab some pizza and head to his place to cheer him up. Or those amazing burgers and fries he loves from the deli."

"It might be nice to just hang out and have a break. It's been a crappy week."

"What's happening?" Will shot a look his way as they headed down the street.

"My lawyer sent the divorce documents to the Baxter's lawyer in Chicago. Tiffany still won't speak to me and her mother told me to take a hike."

"Damn. It never gets any easier, does it?"

"Nope." He sighed. "Let's talk about something else. Even thinking about my life is exhausting."

"Only if you promise not to go MIA again."

Aiden nodded. "Deal."

An hour later, with take-out bags in hand, they arrived at Matthias's apartment building. They rang the buzzer, but there was no answer.

"Now what?" Aiden asked.

"Bill knows us, so maybe he'll let us in, or at least be able to tell us if he's seen the guy." Will tapped on the buzzer for 3C, the outside door buzzing only seconds later.

Aiden shrugged and stepped into the lobby. "So much for security, but we're in." He led the way up to the third floor.

Will tapped on the door. "Hey, Matthias. Open up." He waited for a moment before knocking again. "Matt?"

The door to 3C opened and Bill stuck his head out. "Oh, hey, guys. I haven't seen Matthias for a few days. I thought he'd gone home."

"Not that he told us. He usually mentions it," Will said.

Aiden reached out and grabbed the handle, surprised when it turned easily in his hand. "It's unlocked." He opened the apartment door slowly. "Matthias?" He wrinkled his nose at the stench. "Damn. What in the hell?" After glancing at the other two men, he stepped into the apartment, only managing a few paces inside before he steadied himself against the wall with one hand. "Shit." His knees threatened to buckle as he took in the sight, swallowing hard to fight the ominous sour taste in his mouth. "Call an ambulance."

The words sounded like they were traveling down a long, dark tunnel. Spots danced in front of his eyes as he pressed the back of one hand to his mouth and closed his eyes. It had to be a nightmare.

Will shoved past but came to an abrupt halt only a few inches in front of Aiden, the take-out bags hitting the floor with a hollow thud. "Oh, Matt, what have you done?" He sank to the floor, clutching his head in his hands. "It's too late."

Aiden forced himself to look up at Matthias, his mind fighting to make sense of the scene. Will was right. He'd known it the moment he'd caught sight of his friend dangling from the ceiling. There was nothing they could do. Matthias was beyond any medical aid.

After Bill had ushered them out of the apartment, he called emergency services and invited them to wait inside his place until the police arrived.

Aiden slumped on the couch, unable to move, the pictures of his friend's mottled, lifeless body etched into his brain. The reality was inescapable. He'd failed everyone. His wife and his friends.

If he hadn't spent the last several years wrapped up in himself and his goal to become a doctor, perhaps he wouldn't have driven Tiffany away and missed the signs that led her to the drastic action of overdosing on her mother's pills.

That too was his fault even if they weren't his pills. Their group had many discussions and there had even been several distasteful jokes from some of the members of their group on which medications would provide the quickest pain-free death.

And Matthias. He'd known the guy was struggling with being so far from home and the breakup with Tess, but still, he'd worried more about himself and the crap going on in his own life with little thought to his friend's pain. If he'd gone to see him or invited the man out for a drink instead of wallowing in self-pity, perhaps he could have helped. If he'd hung around Philly on weekends instead of making the trip to New York to continue his liaison with Angelica, Matthias may have talked to him and unloaded his problems.

All the scenarios slogged through his muddled head in a hazy parade of should haves and could haves. About now, someone would be heading to the guy's home to tell his family that their son and brother was dead. A promising life and career had been cut short by the pressures and stress of medical school and losing the love of his life.

Aiden cupped his hands over his face, sucking in long breaths, the endless sitting and answering of questions taking its toll. He pushed to his feet and bolted toward the hall, down the stairs, and out the front door before the nausea rolled over him. He ducked around the corner into the alley, leaning a hand against the rough bricks of the apartment building, unable to hold it back. His virtually empty stomach heaved violently, causing a pain to lance through him.

A warm hand landed on his shoulder. "Hey. Are you okay?" Will asked.

Aiden shook his head as he wiped the back of his hand across his mouth.

"The police are done with the questions for now and they know where to contact us. Why don't you stay at my place tonight? The couch isn't great, but being alone tonight isn't a good idea. Ben is home too."

He gave a brief nod, still unable to speak. The lump in his throat made it impossible to utter a single sound. This day would haunt him forever and as much as he didn't want to talk to anyone, he wouldn't make the mistake of thinking he'd be okay.

And he figured Will needed his company as much as he needed Will's. Friends should stick together at times like these.

He vowed never to make the same mistakes again or put his friends through the same agony currently tearing through his soul. He'd done enough damage to those around him. As difficult as it would be to move on with his life without those he'd lost, he'd do it, one day at a time. One step at a time. He owed it to them. He owed it to himself.

Chapter 28

Tiffany

The inevitable day had arrived. Six months had passed since she'd ended up in the ER in Chicago, feeling like her life was over. And in some ways, that day was the harbinger of her future. Her childhood was over. But thankfully, so were the harsh teenage years, even if they'd been replaced with grown-up responsibilities and realities.

Today she'd end her marriage to the husband she hadn't set eyes on for months. Not since that day in the hospital room in Philly when she'd told him she didn't need him or even want him. It hurt that he'd never bothered to call or visit. His absence made her realize how little she'd meant to him.

Tiffany followed the receptionist into the conference room and sat beside her lawyer, accepting the offered water with a tight smile.

Aiden shifted in his seat but didn't bother to look her way. Instead he stared at his hands and took an occasional sip from his own glass of water.

"Now that both parties are present"—the man beside Aiden cleared his throat—"we can proceed. The details are finalized, so let's get these documents executed. My client has a flight to catch." He slid a copy of the document across the table toward them.

Tiffany's lawyer scanned the document before she turned. "Are you sure you want to sign this? It's only fraction of what you should be getting."

Tiffany nodded, keeping her eyes focused on a spot on the table. She hadn't really wanted anything from Aiden except for her art table, which he'd shipped to her new address. It was her lawyer who'd talked her into accepting a lump sum to pay for her tuition at the Art Institute along with a generous living allowance that provided sufficient funds for her to rent an apartment and declare independence from her parents until she finished her education.

Persuading her mother and father that returning to school and living on her own was a good idea hadn't been easy, but for once, she had an advocate. Their family doctor supported the plan, planting the idea that being self-sufficient was a positive step in Tiffany's recovery. And it was. Her childhood home was suffocating and she was wilting under her mother's watchful eye.

In return, Tiffany promised her doctor she'd attend regular counseling sessions. Not that her parents had a clue about that part of the agreement. Her mother would be horrified at the thought their family secrets would be shared with a total stranger. Her father would probably track the poor woman down and issue threats until the doctor moved her practice to another state.

After an eternity, her lawyer handed her a pen. "There ... there ... and right there. Initial each copy there."

Her pen swished across the paper as she signed away her rights to both Aiden and his fortune. She peered up as her soon-to-be-ex-husband signed each document without a single flicker of regret or emotion.

The moment he was finished, he shook his lawyer's hand and left the room.

So this was how it ended. Without a single word? After everything?

She snatched her coat and purse off the neighboring chair and stalked after him. "Aiden!"

He shot her a look as he pressed the call button for the elevator.

"That's it? You have nothing to say to me?"

"What would you like me to say? See you later?" He crossed his arms. "Your school's paid for and now we can both move on with our lives. You wanted me to leave you alone, and I have." He stepped into the elevator with her only one step behind.

The doors slid shut, cutting them off from the outside world.

"You can't even look at me. Am I that horrible? You made mistakes too, Aiden. The minute we ran into trouble, you left me and—"

"Ran into trouble?" He narrowed his eyes. "Is that how you classify cheating on your husband?"

"And you were oh-so-perfect! What about everything I went through! You were playing around in Europe while I was stuck here. Then I sacrificed my place in one of the best art schools to move to Philly. For you!"

"I won't demand any further sacrifices. Why are you making this difficult? You wanted me out of your life. It's done, so let's move on."

Her anger flashed. "You never wanted the baby, so I guess you won."

"Are you fucking kidding?" He slammed his hand into the red emergency stop button, the alarm engaging. "You think I wished that on you?"

"You didn't want the baby." Tiffany lifted her chin and glared at him. "Now you're off the hook."

He crossed his arms. "How can you blame me? None of it was my fault. But you know what? It was for the best. Can you imagine us raising a kid together? Talk about a disaster waiting to happen. Anyway, that was never going to happen, or haven't you figured that out yet?"

"You're such an asshole." She dabbed at her eyes. "You couldn't wait to run out on me. It sure took you a long time to get over it, with *Angelica*. And all the other women."

"Yeah, it was all me. I'm just the asshole who ruined your life. Whatever." He smacked the button for the main floor, muttering something under his breath that sounded suspiciously like *raging bitch*.

"I never want to see your face, ever again!"

"Done. I've had enough of you and your family. See you never." The doors swished open and he stalked out.

Tiffany took two hesitant steps forward, ignoring the curious gazes of the people pushing past her to enter the elevator. Just like that, it was over. The only man she'd ever loved was gone, along with her dreams of their life together.

But maybe he was right. *Everything we promised was simply an impossible fantasy, an illusion created by two teenagers who thought they understood what true love meant.* Two teenagers who'd grown up the hard way and lost everything in the process.

Today, despite the pain and sadness, she felt grateful. She'd been granted the freedom to move forward on her own terms and finally experience life. Now she would take her next steps into the future, wherever they might lead.

Thank you for reading!

I always love to hear from readers. I can be contacted at http://katesmithauthor.ca

Follow me on social media:

https://www.instagram.com/katesmithauthor/

https://twitter.com/KateSmithAuthor/

https://www.facebook.com/katesmithauthor/

Series Titles

Everything we Lost - Book 1

Everything for Love - Book 2

Never Let You Fall - Book 3

Everything left Unsaid - Book 4

Everything we Dream - Book 5

Everything we Promised - Book 6

Purchase links for these books may be found at KateSmithAuthor.ca

www.ingramcontent.com/pod-product-compliance
Lightning Source LLC
Chambersburg PA
CBHW020532080526
44583CB00013B/834